FINAL HEARING
A NOVEL

BY OSCAR L. SANDERS

ISBN 10: 1515128423

EPUB 13: 9781515128427

Title page and cover design by Oscar Sanders

Table of Contents

CHAPTER ONE

Tomorrow Is a Big Day

Flakes. Snowflakes the size of small rocks blanketed the yard at Great Meadow Correctional Facility. "Comstock," is the name its residents called the prison. It was nearly 2 p.m. and the inmates had just been let outside after afternoon chow. No matter how severe the weather, everyone wanted to be outside—every day. As the men congregated strategically in groups throughout the yard, one man among them, dressed in his "greens", strutted across the baseball field to a bank of pay telephones.

Stress lines outlined Reggie Cochrane's rugged profile. The five-foot, ten inch inmate with the bowed legs and crooked smile needed to keep a close ear on the activities going on outside Comstock's forty foot wall.

"TRYCOM," said the automated female voice that Reggie liked to imagine as a real woman—one he had named Candy. He envisioned her with long brown legs, full, heart-shaped lips, melon-size breasts and soft, round hips. He desperately missed women.

"For collect calls, press one," Candy said. "For credit card billing, press two. For person to person calls, press three."

Reggie pressed the number One. "Please wait for the operator," Candy added.

"TRYCOM. Can I help you?" Reggie was pleasantly surprised by the interjection of a real woman's voice. He cleared his throat and closed his eyes to imagine what she wasn't wearing before he spoke.

"Ahhh...yes, I'd like to make a collect call to the number I just dialed."

"Yes, sir. What's the name?"

"Reggie Cochrane."

"Hold please, Mr. Cochrane, while I check if your party will accept the charges."

"Okay," Reggie answered.

Reggie was the only inmate using the outside phones on such a cold, snowy day. But this was perfect. He needed as much time as this call would take and nobody sweating him to get off the phone because they wanted to make a call, too. Plus, Terry Williams was worth it. He could always count on Terry. Ever since they played summer basketball together when they were kids growing up in the Bronx, Terry had always been there for him. Still, Reggie needed to be sure that their plans were being carried out to the letter. He couldn't afford any mistakes and knew he'd sleep better after getting another assurance from his boy, Terry.

"Hello?"

"Hello. This is TRYCOM. Will you accept the charges from a correctional facility from Reggie Cochrane?"

"Yes, I will," Vivian answered.

"Hey Reggieeee! How you doing?"

Reggie relaxed the grip he had on the phone after hearing the welcoming voice of Terry's wife,

Vivian. Her rich, homey squeals made him feel comforted, like a home cooked Thanksgiving meal, each time he called.

"Tomorrow is the big day for you, huh, Reggie?"

"I gotta tell ya, I don't feel as tense and stressed out as I did in '92," Reggie said. "This is just reappearance. This time I just *know* I'm going home."

"I gotta tell ya, Reggie, I couldn't believe it when Terry told me they denied you parole," she said, her voice cracking a bit.

Reggie was at a loss for words. He felt a pang in his heart when he heard Vivian sniffle.

"Hey, Babe, it's okay. Put Terry on the phone."

"Okay. Okay," she sniffed again. "Hold on, alright?"

"Yeah, sure."

Terry didn't tell him that Viv was so broken up on his being denied parole. All he talked about was the party he and Vivian were planning. They had rented a limo to pick him up. According to Terry, they were sparing no expense.

Terry and Vivian were closer than family for the past ten years of Reggie's sentence.

Reggie had observed that most inmates begin doing their time with only isolation as their primary companion. Family members and friends are left at the front gate, and those doing time have to look for a higher power for support from that point on. Next, Reggie determined that the life of the inmate continues on behind bars, even though his or her life is considerably altered. He noticed that the inmates who continued to develop their minds through reading, writing and learning new skills, had a better chance of not only surviving prison life, but of making it when they got out. He was determined not to let his mind become idle and most of all, not to allow the inhumanity of incarceration to make him a negative person.

Reggie stayed positive by dreaming of the day he'd be released from prison. That was the day his plan, the plan he'd been developing since 1984, would be put into action.

"What's up, Pop?" Terry greeted Reggie the way he always had.

"Hahaaaa, it's good to hear your voice, Bro!" Reggie said.

"Same here. Same here," Terry replied.

"It's that time again," Reggie said.

"Yes, I got it marked on my calendar, Dude!" Terry said. "So what's up?"

"Man, it really looks like I'm going to be released sixty days from tomorrow."

"Excellent, man! That's great, Reg." Terry said. "In fact, I'm meeting with some people that share our interests next week."

"Okay. That's good! Thanks, Man," Reggie replied.

"Yup. And you know I'm just days away from closing on that real estate deal we talked about," Terry said. "It's all coming together. Your vision is taking shape, Bro!" He howled in laughter. "Oh, I forgot to tell you man, I even got the gurney!"

"Yeah? How'd you do that?"

"Man, Viv's girlfriend works at a hospital in the purchasing department. I asked her to hook us up."

"Wow," Reggie said, raising his head toward the sky and playfully allowing the now softer snowflakes to moisten the smile on his face. He looked around the yard at his colleagues—some three to four thousand men. Some walking. Some working out. Some smoking. But not one with a plan.

"Reggie, did you hear me?"

"Yeah, of course, man. I can't believe how smooth things are going. You know?"

"Yeah. Me too," Terry added "So far, so good."

As Reggie hung up the jack and spun around to join the others in the yard, he was surprised to find a prison guard standing toe to toe, right in front of him.

"Damn, what's up?"

"Parole wants to see you Cochran," the guard replied.

"Cool, let's do this," Reggie said, strolling ahead of the guard. The briskness of his step exuded the confidence of a man who could nearly taste his freedom.

As Reggie walked through the yard, other inmates hit him with affirming comments about his soon-to-be-release. Several inmates made a gauntlet for him to pass through.

"Hey Reggie, I know it feels good to be a short-timer," called out one inmate.

"Give 'em hell when you get out there, Cochran," shouted another.

With a clinched fist, Reggie tapped his heart and then raised the peace sign above his head. "I'll rap to you guys later," he said.

This was typical. People always reacted to Reggie Cochran with respect—even here in jail. From day-one, Reggie was revered. After all, his case was a famous one.

CHAPTER TWO

Parole Granted

A woman and two men dressed in business suits marched into the administrative offices of Comstock. They each were dragging portable file cabinets into the meeting room in preparation for various parole hearings they were scheduled to preside over today. The first of which was Reggie Cochrane's.

Awaiting the chow bell, Reggie paced in his cell. He had been up half the night. He was almost finished reading *The Way It Really Is*, a book by David Fuller that most inmates about to be released read like a Bible. He had only 15 pages left, but he couldn't concentrate—not today.

Once in the chow hall, Reggie tried to act nonchalant. He didn't want his colleagues to peep his card. He was actually happy for the first time in ten years. Happiness felt strange to him. Typically he was moody and standoffish. Today, he wanted to do back flips, somersaults and full out break dance right in the middle of the floor. Instead, he took his usual spot in the last row of the chow hall, all the way in the back, all alone.

Reggie said a prayer before digging into his breakfast. He stifled a smile when Bo, a burglar from Detroit, also convicted and sentenced to ten years hard time, began acting out. Bo was crazy as hell, but harmless. He was an accidental comedian, giving the inmates improv shows whenever his meds needed adjusting or if he had sold the last dosage and needed another one to keep his head on straight. Today Bo went over to the window, held his tray over his head and started shaking his head and ass from left to right. He rolled his big, pop eyes around, licked his lips and stuck out his tongue like a snake. When the C.O.s approached him, Bo threw his food tray at them and began tearing off his clothes before they took him down.

Reggie allowed himself a brief chuckle. He would miss Bo. Other than being certified nuts, Bo was a good dude. Mostly quiet like Reggie and just doing his time the best way he could.

After the guards took Bo out, half-naked and kicking and screaming for his Mama, the usual chow hall sounds returned. Reggie took it all in. He watched the men greeting each other, laughing, talking about old times and eating. The guards' radios offered a low buzz reminder that it was a typical day at Comstock—nothing exciting, just typical employee communications.

Reggie looked around remembering his first day there noticing the chipped and dirty walls and ceiling. It was a long time since he had even looked at those walls. And then, it was only when the guards put up a corny new poster encouraging the inmates to 'Think Responsibly' or that 'Respect is an Inside Job that Starts in Your Heart.' It reminded him of the way foreign jails looked in the movies, with the ceilings cracking and paint chips falling into inmates' food.

Reggie couldn't wait to get out of this place. He was supposed to get out in 1992 but those dirty bastards held him back. They knew he would bounce back quickly, thanks to his brother Vinnie's contacts down at City Hall. Reggie figured he'd have to work for a while until he got on his feet and then he'd move on. He wanted to help inmates nationwide to keep their rights from being violated by starting an advocacy group. But until that time, Reggie would have to hold his tongue and be humble. He needed to remain mindful of the people who held the key to his pending emancipation.

It was an unwritten rule among the inmate that anyone going before the parole commission were to allow them to set you straight if you want to be released. The idea was to be cordial and respectful to the commissioners. After all, they held an inmate's destiny in their hands. Now it was Reggie's turn.

Parole officers from the facility were also in attendance, sitting in rows of seats behind Reggie's ringside seat before the commissioners. Reggie ignored them. To him, they were nothing but window dressing, like the croutons on the salad or the salt on the rim of the margarita glass. They served no real purpose in the outcome of his case. That left Reggie in the middle, right where he wanted be.

"Mr. Cochran? One of the commissioners noticed Reggie's mind wandering.

"Yes," Reggie answered.

"I guess you know why you're here."

"Yes I do."

"This is your parole hearing where it will be determined if you will be released from this correctional facility."

"I think you got it all wrong Commish," Reggie said, smiling. "I think you better check your records because I have served two-thirds of my time. Now you have no choice but to kick the gate open and let me the fuck out, ya' dig."

The Commissioner cleared his throat. "Are you done, Mr. Cochrane?" he asked.

"I'm done."

"Great," the Commissioner said flatly. "Then if it's okay with you, I'd like to proceed.

"Me too," Reggie added leaning forward in his chair.

"This is your parole hearing. My name is Thomas Boyle. To my left is Cynthia Howarth and this is Mr. DeMello," he added and pointed to his right.

"I'll be asking the questions." Boyle said.

"Okay, let's do it," Reggie said, scratching the side of his face.

"On July 17, 1984, you were convicted of arson in the second degree. What the hell were you thinking about when you committed that vicious crime?"

"I can sum it up in one word—revenge. Reggie said calmly. "My brother was on trial for bribery. And I didn't believe he was being defended to the fullest extent of the law. That's my personal take on that."

"Mr. Cochrane, let me ask you this: who appointed you God?" Boyle asked, crossing his arms in front of his chest.

"No one sir. But where my brother is concerned I have a vested interest, that's all."

"You have a vested interest?" Boyle asked.

"Yes."

"*You* have a vested interest?" Boyle repeated louder.

Reggie let Boyle's voice settle in the room. He fought back the temptation to spit in Boyle's face, sitting as still as a statute staring at the Commissioner's pasty face. This reminded Reggie of Nuremberg—and like he was living through a third inquisition, including his original conviction in 1984.

"Stenographer, did you get Mr. Cochrane's last answer?" Commissioner Cynthia Howarth's high-pitched voice broke the palatable silence in the room.

"Yes, ma'am," the woman said.

"Talk more about your vested interest, Mr. Cochrane," Boyle instructed.

"It's really nothing to talk about," Reggie added, sitting back in the chair. "When this whole incident jumped off, I thought it was the end of my brother's political career. He had worked so fucking hard and built such a positive reputation. And to see someone take it all away—man, it felt to me like my brother's career was totally over. And I knew that the case against him was weak as hell. They had trumped up all these bogus charges against him. Vinnie was the fall guy, that's all."

"Was this information available to your brother and his lawyer at the time of his trial or appeal?" Boyle asked—his tone notably softer.

"Oh yeah," Reggie answered, looking down at his now clasped hands. "Everything was available. You just don't get it," he added, shaking his head as if to ward off the memory of a nightmare. "This was the trial of the decade. Vinnie had to go down—it was as simple as that."

"Was he in too deep?" DeMello asked.

"Who?"

"Your brother."

"What does any of this have to do with my parole hearing?" Reggie replied, sucking his teeth.

"Uh...I agree," Boyle answered. "Let's get back to Mr. Cochrane's hearing."

Turning his attention back to Reggie, he asked, "By the way, where will you live when you are released?"

"With my ex-wife."

"Do you have employment lined up?" Howarth interjected.

"I haven't lined up work yet. But that's not a problem. If push comes to shove, I'll work with my brother Vinnie."

"What lesson have you learned from your stay here?" Boyle asked, tapping his pen lightly on the notebook in front of him.

Reggie looked up at the ceiling for a moment before answering. "Prison is a place for redemption and I've certainly redeemed myself. I'm not gonna make a speech on the subject, but I can guarantee you this—I won't be back."

"I certainly hope that's true, Mr. Cochrane. Unfortunately, nothing in life is guaranteed." The three commissioners looked at each other and shared a laugh at Reggie's expense.

"I'll tell you what," Reggie said loud enough to get them to re-focus, "I will personally invite all of you to a celebration dinner where I will give you a status report."

An awkward pause settled over the commissioners. "Sorry, Mr. Cochrane, but we can't accept a dinner invitation from you in good faith."

"I know. I know," Reggie said, waving his hand in front of his face. "It's a policy thing. I understand. But I would love the opportunity to show you that I definitely will not be returning to prison."

Boyle put down his pen and leaned forward, his chest pressing against the table in front of him. "Let me give you a piece of advice, Mr. Cochran. Just do the right thing. I think you have great potential. You just have to apply yourself to positive endeavors when you are released."

"Oh don't worry, I'm gonna make you so proud of me," Reggie said with a devilish smile. "I'll work hard to catch up to you three, 'cause I know you're moving on to bigger and better things."

"You sound pretty sure about that," Howarth stated, looking at Reggie curiously, as if he didn't quite believe what he was hearing.

"Oh yeah!" said Reggie. "Bigger and better," and he repeated as the guards led him out of the hearing.

Silence engulfed the room after the door clicked shut. There was no doubt that Reggie Cochrane had left those parole commissioners confused about his intentions. And that was exactly the way he wanted it.

Exactly two months later, Comstock's iron bars swung open and the toe of a black suede loafer emerged from the darkness. Accompanied by Reverend Lonnie Haskell, Prison Chaplain at Great Meadow, Reggie Cochrane was finally leaving his court-appointed penal vacuum.

Stopping abruptly and grabbing Reggie's shoulders, Reverend Haskell looked into the former inmate's eye. "Reggie, I hope you stick with your plan."

"What plans are you talking about, Rev.?"

"You know. What we talked about—working with your brother, Vincent."

"Rev., I don't worry about me, man. If I have to do that I will. Okay?" Reggie assured the pastor. "I just got a lot on my mind right now."

"Like what Reggie? You used to talk to me." Rev Haskell said.

"Please, Rev. I'm almost outta here. I gotta few things in the works. You don't need to worry about me anymore."

"This is not just about my job here Reggie," Reverend Haskell said. "I care about what happens to you, but you shut me out of your plans for the future."

"Come on, man," Reggie said. "This ain't the time. You know I don't talk. I'm not a talker. I'm a doer. When I came here, my policy was to keep my mouth shut and my ears open until I left and that's exactly what I did. Real talk, Rev., I'm not feeling like talking about my plans right now."

"Okay. Okay," Reverend Haskell lifted both hands in surrender. "Just know that you can always call me if you ever do want to talk."

Reggie gave the pastor a pound and they continued down the corridor in silence. The two men shook hands and hugged one last time. Reggie wondered why the Reverend was so interested in his life. *'Is this guy some kind of prison spy?'* he thought.

Reverend Haskell left Reggie at the property desk, where the now freed inmate retrieved a large brown envelope containing all his earthly belongings—namely, a watch, wallet, a pink slip voucher attached to a legal envelope containing five thousand dollars that Vinnie had put into his account.

Reggie felt strange walking through the prison doors without handcuffs and unattended, but the odd feeling helped Reggie to truly believe he was finally free. He smiled as the sun glare pierced his eyes and heart as he walked toward Terry's SUV on the left side of the parking lot. He could see that Terry's wife, Vivian, was with him in the black Toyota Four-Runner.

When Reggie approached the SUV, he could hear the delicate sounds of Toni Braxton creating an atmosphere of relaxation that he hadn't felt for the past ten years. The two front doors flung open and Terry and Vivian got out yelling in unison, "Hey!" And the three friends embraced tearfully.

"Damn, you look good, man," Terry said wiping the tears from his eyes.

"Thanks, man." Reggie said.

"Yeah, Reggie," Vivian added. "You look younger now than you did when you came here. Now how did you manage that?"

"Aaaaahhhhh...ancient Chinese secret," Reggie said.

"I'm serious," Vivian said. "You look like a baby!"

"Viv, I just stayed to my fucking self, did my time and, God damn it, here I am—ready to strike like a viper!"

"Yeah. A *baby* viper," Viv joked.

The three friends laughed heartedly as they entered the Runner and sped off. They were driving south, heading for New York City. Once they were cruising comfortably along the highway, Terry began describing the progress he had made so far.

"Sheldon Weinstock was the agent that assisted me from application to closing," he explained to Reggie, looking at him through the rearview mirror. "We just closed nine days ago. Sheldon was very helpful in securing the chateau."

"Alright. Good to know," Reggie said.

"Each time we met, Sheldon insisted on taking me out to lunch," Terry added.

"Maybe that's what he does for all his clients who shell out $1.7 million," he said with a chuckle.

"$1.7 million? Isn't that kinda cheap for a chateau?"

"It is, but he couldn't get the $9 million the seller was originally asking for. You see, I did some digging and found out that a doctor killed his whole family in that big ass house. Nobody wanted it so I chiseled him down to *my* price."

"Whoa! You did your homework on that one. And he was a decent guy about it? Sounds like you enjoyed doing business with him."

"I enjoy doing business with anybody who gives me what the fuck I want and picks up the check on top of that." Terry said as Reggie and Vivian shared a laugh.

"Yeah, that's my man," Reggie added, rubbing Terry on the shoulder as he drove.

"How 'bout the props? Did you have any trouble obtaining the equipment we need to set up the operation?" Reggie asked.

"No. No problems at all. Matter of fact, I had Thompson—"

"You mean the C.O. at Comstock?" Reggie interrupted.

"Yeah. He was real helpful, too, man." Terry said nodding his head. "I had to have stuff shipped from Utah. Thompson knew about a place that would let me place an order and have it shipped to me anywhere in the country—no questions asked."

"So, Thompson is cool, huh? I never talked to his ass personally," Reggie said, checking out the scenery along the highway.

"I had him checked out by people I know at the F.B.I. He's the real deal, believe me!" Terry declared as he swerved between cars on his way to his destination. "He has connections all over the world. He's our man." Terry said.

"I'm sorry," Reggie said. "But you know he may have to be snuffed out at some point."

"I don't care," Terry said, sucking his teeth. "I guess you feel that way because he knows too much about our plan, right?"

"Precisely," Reggie answered. "I just want to be sure that feelings don't get in the way."

"Fuck 'em. He's no friend of mine," Terry said.

Reggie made eye contact with Terry through the rear view mirror and said, "Good. It's critical that we stay focused."

Terry was like a brother to Reggie. But he had learned years ago that Terry was too trusting. The two friends met at the Harlem Y.M.C.A. when they both were 17 years old. They were a back court tandem that gave opposing teams a hard way to go. Together they would average 41 points, 11 assists, and seven steals per game for the four years they played together at Harlem Y.

Then, just as fate had brought them together, destiny separated them. Somehow Terry's name was left off the Y's roster. Unfortunately, their fifth summer as a duo was not meant to be. Terry wound up joining Minisink Townhouse and marched them to the finals in the Holcombe Rucker Summer Tournament against Stone Gym.

Reggie was happy for Terry when Minisink went to the finals and subsequently won the championship. It was an achievement that Reggie never enjoyed. Whenever Terry and Reggie walked the streets, people rushed over to congratulate Terry. This bothered Reggie at times, but he dealt with it. After all, Terry was his boy, no matter what.

A couple of years later, on a cool spring afternoon, as Terry waited for a bus; he was joined by an elderly man. They smiled at each other until the old man asked, "How long you been waiting?"

"You talking to me?" Terry asked.

"Yes," the man repeated, "How long you been waiting for the bus?"

"Not long. Actually, I just got here before you did."

"Okay," the man said. "I'll tell you, young man, it's no joke getting old," the old man added. "I'm tired. I've been carrying this heavy bag all day."

"Why don't you put it down?" Terry asked. "It might be a while before the bus gets here. Rest the bag for a minute."

The old man put the bag down. "Young brother, is there a store around here? I need to buy a pack of cigarettes."

"Oh yeah," Terry said. "It's just around this corner," he pointed in the store's direction. "I'll watch your bag for you."

"You'd do that for me?"

"Yeah. No problem," Terry said, smiling at the old dude.

"Okay. I'll make it quick," the old man said.

The septuagenarian scurried around the corner and Terry slid the bag closer to him. About a minute passed before Terry noticed that the bus was approaching. He looked behind him to see if he saw the old man coming, but he was nowhere in sight. Terry didn't want to leave the bag unattended. He kept checking to see if the old man was coming, but he didn't appear.

When the bus pulled up to the stop, Terry picked up the bag and walked to the corner with it. Still, the old man was nowhere to be seen. Terry decided to take the bag with him and drop it off at the precinct near his home.

After only two stops, two men entered the bus and walked directly over to where he was sitting.

"Excuse me, Pal, is that your bag?" one of the men asked pointing to the bag.

"Who are you?" Terry asked.

"We're NYPD Detectives," one of the men answered as they both flashed their badges in front of Terry's face.

"Well, is it?" the second detective inquired.

"Is what?" Terry asked.

"Look, is this goddamn bag yours?" the stockier of the two detectives said.

Nah...I was just watching it for this old dude who was waiting at the bus stop with me," Terry explained.

"Okay. Where is this old dude? The stocky detective asked Terry.

"He said he was going to the store, but he didn't come back," Terry said.

The two detectives grabbed Terry by each arm and lifted him out of his seat.

"Yo! Yo!" he yelled. "Get your hands off me, man. That old bastard set me up! What's in that bag? Yo! This ain't fair. I was just trying to help that old mother fucker. Now he's gone and I have to take the weight?"

The other passengers on the bus looked away as Terry was dragged off the bus.

Terry repeated history to the two detectives after they read him his rights and put him into the patrol car that was following the bus. He also told it to anyone who'd listen once they booked him at the precinct, but the detectives had observed Terry assume responsibility for the bag at the bus stop and board the bus with it. They had been following the old man, a known marijuana trafficker, and they believed Terry to be just another mule.

The police charged him with possession of marijuana in the fifth degree—a "Class A" misdemeanor. When all was said and done, the D.A.'s office offered Terry a sentence of one-year probation, in exchange for his guilty plea, since Terry had no prior criminal record.

After Reggie heard about Terry's dilemma, he made a mental note to always question Terry's trust of people—especially those he really didn't know. And this included C.O. Thompson, too. Reggie didn't trust anybody. Period!

CHAPTER THREE

A Chateau with a Purpose

Barreling down Interstate 4 toward Albany, Reggie sat back and enjoyed the scenery since they had a long ride ahead of them. Weather-aged farmhouses spread out amongst the plains. Apple orchards lay bare with branches bent like scarecrows. The sky was a warm robin's egg blue, dotted with exploding white clouds. There were points during the drive when Reggie's eye only followed the thin yellow line separating one side of the road from the other. It reminded him that they were getting closer and closer to their destination. After his long stint at Comstock, he now appreciated such simple treasures.

"What's the name of the place we're heading, again?" he asked.

"A town outside of Albany called Minands." Terry replied.

"Is that where the chateau is located?"

"Yup. The contractors are working as we speak. They're renovating the place to our specifications," Terry said. "I figure we would take a spin by the place to check it out."

"Yeah, that sounds good," Reggie said. "But when will I see Jaco?"

"Jaco is overseeing the work at the chateau," Terry explained. "Nobody has lived in there for years. Some guy—a teacher—murdered his wife and seven children there. That's why I was able to get it so cheap. Don't worry, man. You'll see Jaco when we get to Minands."

Vivian stroked Terry's cheek with her long nails. "Honey, let's find somewhere to stop. I have to use the Lady's Room."

Terry smiled at his wife and began veering toward the highway's exit. When they arrived at the rest area, Vivian bolted from the vehicle and rushed inside. Terry's phone rang as the two men were getting out of the truck.

"Yeah, this is Terry, go on. Uh-uh. I don't understand. Did they leave enough paint and cleaning materials? Oh, okay," he said. "You got me nervous for a moment there," he added as Reggie looked on curiously. "Hey, I'm on my way there now. I'm bringing somebody with me. You'll see who it is when I get there, Jaco. We'll see you soon."

Jaco Philips was the final team member. By far, he was the best man to handle the mounting responsibilities of this initiative. A former Vietnam veteran, Jaco joined the Black Panthers in 1971 back in his hometown of Philadelphia.

Jaco was unassuming as a torture practitioner. He was average height—about five foot-eight. He sported a shiny bald head, was slim, except for his chiseled, barrel-chest and was awkwardly pigeon-toed. No one would have guessed that Jaco had traveled extensively throughout the Middle East or that he had been hired extensively to mutilate individuals thought to be spies or political malcontents on behalf of Islamic governments. Various confidential documents named those governments to include Lebanon, Syria, Iran, and Yemen among others.

Blanket denial was the position of every government alleged to have solicited his services. And Jaco's family and friends had no knowledge of what Jaco actually did for a living. And even under the most vicious torture, Jaco never, ever admitted to his background. Jaco was just the kind of man Reggie needed on this project.

Terry met Jaco in London at Wembley Stadium, where they were fans of British heavyweight boxing champion Simon Davis. Davis was managed by a man named Baron Von Mickva, renowned in boxing circles for turning club fighters into champions. His fighter, Davis, had won an easy decision over Park Cahill.

After the bout, an usher approached Terry and informed him that the Baron wanted to have a word with him in his stadium office. The usher led the way as they entered the elevator and rode to the fourth floor. When the door opened, Terry's eyes were treated to an expansive Italian marble floor and beautiful white leather sofas and chairs.

Terry noticed the Baron standing against a huge glass window behind a cherry wood desk stacked with portfolios. A second well-dressed man sat stoically in a chair to the right of the desk.

"Welcome. Have a seat," Von Mickva said.

Terry pulled up a chair and sat down, feeling as uncomfortable as a midget among giants.

"You're the man that manages Simon Davis, right? Terry asked.

"Ah...I take it you are a fan of the sweet science," Von Mickva said. "I am Baron Von Mickva and this gentleman is my close associate, Jaco Philips," he said, waving towards Jaco.

"My name is Williams-Terry Williams," Terry stammered. "Forgive me, but I'm a little confused about why you asked to meet me."

"Understandably so," Von Mickva said laughing. "I'll get right to the point, Mr. Williams. My associate here, Jaco, has informed me of your friend's one-time publicized life and I am prepared to extend my influence to you."

"I'm sorry," Terry said, getting up to leave. "I don't know what you're talking about. Maybe you guys have me confused with someone else. "

"Wait, Mr. Williams," Jaco chimed in. "Let me explain. I was in New York City in 1984—July to be exact. I had been there for three months. During my stay, your friend, Reggie Cochran was all over the newspapers. I felt for the guy-I really did. He thought his brother was getting the shaft and he wanted to get involved," Jaco said. "And boy, did he get involved!"

"I'm not going to discuss that with you," Terry responded defensively.

"You feel for him don't you?" Von Mickva asked, moving toward Terry.

"Yeah. Of course I do," Terry answered. "We grew up together playing ball in the streets. What happened to Reggie shouldn't have happened. Reggie is a standup guy—always has been and he stood up for his brother," Terry said.

"Mr. Williams, I commend your lifelong friendship with Reggie Cochran. I find it admirable and refreshing at the same time. May I invite you to join us for dinner?" Von Mickva asked.

"I don't know, it's late and all, you know," Terry said.

"Please. I insist," Von Mickva said. "There's a restaurant only about a mile from here. After dinner, my driver will take you anywhere you want to go.

"Okay," Terry said, shrugging his shoulders. But is it okay if I use your telephone first?"

"Absolutely," Von Mickva said, pointing to the telephone on his desk. "The telephone is there and Jaco and I will be waiting in the parking lot. Take your time, Mr. Williams," he added.

At a table reserved at the famous London restaurant, Jerry Snowdens, Von Mickva and Jaco resumed their conversation with Terry.

"Why didn't you bring your wife?" Jaco probed.

"She's not a boxing fan," answered Terry. "That's too bad," Jaco said.

"I'm curious. How do you know I'm married?" Terry asked.

"I was at the trial and I saw you there with your wife, Vivian, I think I heard you call her. Am I right?"

Terry nodded.

"She's a very attractive woman. You're lucky to have her," Jaco said tilting his upraised wine glass in Terry's direction.

"I don't remember calling her my wife," Terry said.

"That's what was reported in the newspapers when the two of you were at the trial," Jaco answered.

Terry put his fork down. "It seems you know a lot about Reggie and his brother, Vincent's cases. You even know a few things about me. What? Are you guys writing a book or something?" Terry asked glaring at Jaco and Von Mickva.

"Not at all, Mr. Williams. I can assure you, I'm not writing a book," Von Mickva said. "Let me assure you that we're on your side. I have privately financed attacks on government buildings and employees, merely to terrorize certain agencies for the political positions taken on behalf of so-called allies-United Nations mostly. Jaco fulfills my orders by enlisting private contractors to carry out my directives," Von Mickva continued. "I realize that the court system has wronged your friend, his brother and even you when they charged you with possession of marijuana when you were a teenager," Von Mickva explained.

Terry grinned, impressed with the Baron's and Jaco's grasp of the personal history of Reggie, Vincent and himself. They had peaked his interest in finding out just how much these two men could do for them in the near future.

"We've done our homework, Mr. Williams. We don't fuck around," Von Mickva said. "Just say the word. Let me know when you and your friends are ready." Von Mickva said.

"Ready for what?" asked Terry

"Think about it," Jaco said. "Just think about it."

"Reggie won't be released for another couple of years," Terry said.

"We're well aware of that," The Baron said, taking another sip of wine. "We simply wanted you to know what resources are available when the time comes."

"As soon as Reggie expresses real interest along the lines you're speaking of, I'll be sure to bring him up to speed on your offer."

Von Mickva pursed his lips. He wasn't used to people making him wait, but he smiled and continued dinner as if the three men were good friends.

The following morning, at Heathrow Airport, as Terry headed home, the entire puzzle came together. Terry had been blessed with a golden egg. He had been scouted out by a philanthropist willing to underwrite a project Reggie would likely go for.

When he received Reggie's call a few days after he arrived back home in New York City, he told his friend about Jaco and The Baron's proposition. Reggie was truly intrigued by the news and wanted Terry to stay in touch with the two men. This would make it easier to coordinate their efforts when the time came for Reggie to be released.

Terry was certain to call The Baron twice a year— either in London or at his Las Vegas offices. In 1992, everyone was almost sure that Reggie would be released, so the Baron sent Jaco to New York City to deposit $4.6 million in a shell account under the name Sure West Ltd. The money was to be made available to Reggie and Terry when Reggie was released. When they received the unfortunate news that Reggie's parole was denied, The Baron exercised his patience for two more years.

Back in the rest area, after Vivian refreshed herself, Reggie couldn't help noticing her stunning beauty and sexy strut.

"Yo, man. We've got to get you some ass soon because you're staring at my wife kinda hard," Terry said.

"Now-now baby, if Reggie looks at me, it ain't nothing but a compliment, you know that," Vivian sang out cheerfully. "You and Reggie have been friends since dirt was a baby and he has never shown me anything other than respect, so knock it off. Okay?"

"You're right, Viv," Terry said. "I don't know what got into me. I'm sorry, Reggie," he added, connecting eye to eye with Reggie and extending his hand to his friend "It's all the pressure, I guess."

"Ah, come on man," Reggie said. "I took no offense to that. Besides we gotta peep out that chateau, right?"

Terry nodded and with that they were off again to their next destination.

The scenery was absolutely a panoramic wonder. The view of the mountains and colossal farms were a pleasant distraction from the prior drama that transpired. Soon, the Runner passed a sign that read WELCOME TO MENANDS. They made a right turn at the exit and drove into town.

"Look for a huge house with gates around it and construction trucks parked in the driveway," Terry said.

Reggie was quick to find the chateau because of its large size and tall wrought-iron gate. He had instructed Terry to find a place that commanded a certain amount of privacy-the kind of privacy needed to isolate their guests from nosey neighbors.

They arrived in time to observe Jaco giving instructions to workers outside the house. Dressed in a denim shirt and navy blue slacks, Jaco followed the Runner up the driveway until it came to a complete stop.

"I know, Terry," Jaco said as he paused and gave his visitor the once over, "but you, you must be Reggie Cochran."

Reggie and Jaco shook hands.

"Man, it's a sho'nuff a pleasure to meet you—I mean you had those newspapers writing about you, I'm tellin' you, Reggie-you don't mind me calling' you Reggie, huh?"

"Of course not, but they didn't just write about me though," Reggie said.

"Oh, I know. They also wrote about your brother, Vincent. They called him the linchpin to you guys' insertion into political crime history." Jaco stopped talking when he noticed Vivian.

"Hello. I am Vivian, Terry's wife," she said, displaying a broad, wholesome smile.

"Very nice to meet you," Jaco said. "Your husband tells me that you're not too keen on boxing. Is that true?"

"Where did you hear that?"

Jaco peered over at Terry with a clever smirk on his face, as if to imply an inside joke. They all walked toward the front door, observing the workers making personal observations to one another.

"Let's get down to business, Mr. Cochran," Jaco said. "This place you have here is going to be built to the specifications Terry requested on your behalf. Let me show you around."

On the inside of the chateau antique furniture was being positioned by workers, while expressive African American artwork adorned the walls. An eight-foot Venus de Milo-type statuette spouted water in the center of the foyer area.

Jaco led everyone up the winding staircase that led to the bedrooms.

"There are six bedrooms in this place. A few of the rooms are not finished yet. The rest of the stuff will be here next week," Jaco informed the three of them as Vivian stuck her head in one of the bathrooms to check out the decor.

"The three bathrooms are in working order so no one should have to wait," Jaco added.

"I hope the water doesn't turn cold in the middle of your shower," Vivian said, laughing.

"No-no," Jaco explained. "Here, everything is temperature controlled." He pointed to the control system affixed to the bathroom's Italian marble tiling.

"Nice, very nice," Vivian pronounced slowly. She was silenced by the sudden disappearance of everyone else on the house tour.

"Vivian?" Jaco's unfamiliar voice called out.

"Where are you guys?"

"Over here!"

Vivian walked down the opposite side of the hallway and saw everyone standing patiently inside a secret elevator that led to the cellar, where special rooms are located. Soon, the elevator came to a stop. The doors opened and everyone exited.

The dark, spooky cellar reminded Vivian of the Haunted Mansion amusement park. And the cellar's temperature was lowered to thirty-five degrees to increase the level of fear imposed on guests who visit this level.

Vivian stayed very close to Terry as they walked down the hall. Jaco led them through the cellar to three rooms designated for torture.

"This is where all the shit will end!" Jaco said.

"Can we go inside?" Reggie asked.

"Be my guest, please," Jaco urged, motioning his arm to corral everyone into the room.

Jaco explained that the workers had soundproofed the rooms to mute the pain and terror inflicted on those chosen to endure it from the ears of nosey neighbors.

"It's gonna take at least two and a half months to finish up this place," Jaco explained. "That means all the power will be working and every device will be installed."

"When will the Baron be in New York?" Reggie asked.

"He will be in the U.S., Las Vegas to be specific, in four weeks for a press conference," Jaco reported. "He wants to meet with you while he's here. In the meantime, that gives you a couple of weeks to get acquainted with your freedom. Have fun, Mr.

Cochran, because when everything is in place, you're not gonna have much time for leisure."

"I agree," Reggie said. "Besides, I have a few loose ends to tie up anyway."

Satisfied at the progress of the chateau, Terry, Vivian, and Reggie headed back to New York City.

CHAPTER FOUR

The Matter of Sylvia Mitchell

Terry and Vivian were absolutely mum about the shindig at The Vox, which was just about the most happening night spot in New York City. The club, located in lower Manhattan, was best known for showcasing half-naked women dancing in oversized birdcages hung from the ceiling. If that wasn't enough, The Vox also held a wet panties contest every Tuesday night. That idea came by way of a former patron who was now the club's owner.

Sylvia Mitchell, a former super model, had purchased The Vox a year prior. She had been retired three years now after her arrogance and drug abuse drove her from the high-class covers of *ELITE* and *Mirabella* and onto the scandal-filled pages of *The Star* and *The National Inquirer.* The tawdry tabloids left no stone unturned. Every detail of Sylvia's downfall was exposed. After the papers got finished assassinating her, Sylvia quit modeling and, in 1991, entered a residential drug rehab in Minnesota for ten months.

Some people, even some of her friends, thought Sylvia had died. She disappeared from the scene, choosing only to communicate with certain individuals until she felt strong enough to handle everyday bullshit. Only one person remained a constant positive influence in Sylvia's life—that was Reggie Cochran.

After Sylvia and Reggie became lovers in 1982, she moved into his Bronx apartment. Reggie and Sylvia met at the Whitney Museum. He was attending a party there with his brother, Vincent, then a Bronx councilman. Reggie and Sylvia hit it off immediately. She was constantly turned on by Reggie's sexual spontaneity. He could always come up with the most unique places for making love—like in the fitting room at Barney's or in a stall in the Men's Room at the New York Stock Exchange. For once in Sylvia's life she was happily in love. She felt like a school girl, but one who was free to live out all her sexual fantasies.

Reggie and Sylvia were married in 1983 in an elaborate ceremony and honeymooned in France. Her modeling career was booming and she was finally in love. She had the best of both worlds, but it all came to a sudden end.

First, her brother-in-law, Vincent was arrested and sent to jail. Then, her husband Reggie was pinched. She quickly turned to drugs and alcohol to deal with the stress of these challenges.

Tonight was different. She had left the life of a drug fiend far behind her. Tonight she was hosting a who's who of important people for Reggie's coming home party. Vincent had organized the event and his people along with some celebrities had promised to drop by the club to welcome him home.

"Hey, Reggie good to see ya', man," said Howard Winston, vice president of international accounts for Safra National Bank. Winston flew in from Monaco simply because Vinnie had asked him to.

Simon Davis, the British-born WBA heavyweight boxing champion was also in attendance, as well as several friends from Reggie's childhood. Finally, Vinnie stepped out of the crowd to give his brother a hug.

"Well-well-well, I've been waiting for this moment for a long time," Vinnie said.

"Me too, Bro. Me too! Reggie smiled from ear to ear. "Yo, man, they tell me you arranged all this?"

"Of course. Nothing's too good for my brother. I mean you went all out for me," Vinnie said. "I owe you much more than this."

"Aw, come on, man. That was ten years ago," Reggie said.

"I know, I know. I just wish I could have done more, Reg," Vinnie added. "Believe me, Bro, I wanted to visit you, but, after I got out of jail the media followed me everywhere I went. I didn't want to make you part of that circus. That's why I limited communications to writing you letters."

"Yeah. I remember one of your letters. You said you were laying low and that you had been out for almost four years. Was that because of the press?" Reggie asked, one eyebrow raised as he glared at his brother.

"Yup. No one would take a chance on an ex-convict civil servant who had become the point man for the 17th council district by virtue of a special election," Vinnie said, his jaw tightening. "Man, I disgraced my constituency and myself. I even dragged you into this shit, too, Bro and that was messed up, real messed up."

"Whoa-whoa-whoa. Wait a minute," Reggie said, lowering his voice to avoid raising the interest of nosey onlookers. "I made the decision to get involved. I developed the plan and I hired the manpower. It was me who had stepped into the squared circle. You're my brother. I would've done it anyway."

"Hey, Bro, I'm just glad no one was in the law firm when it burnt down or I wouldn't be talking to you right now," Vinnie said. "I know that."

"When all that shit was going down big brother, frankly, I didn't give a fuck one way or the other," Reggie said.

Suddenly, a female voice broke through the love fest Vinnie and Reggie were sharing. "Would you have done that for me?" Sylvia asked mockingly, keeping a safe distance, but within earshot of the brothers. She sauntered over to Vinnie and Reggie.

"Sylvia!" Reggie said, standing up to give her a big hug. "Damn it's good to see you. Whatcha' mean? Would I do what for you?"

"Burn down a building," Sylvia said, batting her false eyelashes rapidly. "If I had a problem with the people that worked there. Would you burn down a building for me?"

"Uh-uh, Sylvia, I don't think this is the time or the place for that kind of joke," Vinnie said. "Would you like to join us?"

"Why, thank you," she purred and poked out her tits and butt to take a seat in the chair between them.

"And, Vincent, you're looking well," Sylvia sang out.

"Thank you," Vinnie said, looking at the crowd in the room. "And you're looking as beautiful as always, Sylvia," he added. "Every man in the room has at least one eye on you."

"True. I already knew that," Sylvia laughed. "No, really—I'm just bullshitting you. I'm not like that."

Reggie lowered his head and lifted his eyelids upward, "Like what?"

Vinnie took this as an opportunity to excuse himself from the table to join his wife, Nia, in the game room. He could feel the tension between Sylvia and Reggie rising and he thought it was a good time to split.

"When we were together, I thought I knew what I wanted," Sylvia said to Reggie suddenly. "Everyone told me that I was on the right track. Even my parents thought I was making the right decisions. Modeling was my life. Besides that, I had you, which in my heart of hearts, I didn't believe I deserved," she continued, her eyes welling up with tears.

"Sylvia, you're way too hard on yourself," Reggie said, squeezing her hand. "Sometimes relationships are like a great meal—they're just not meant to last."

"No, no, now let me finish. I have to finish," Sylvia said, pulling her hand away. "You never let me finish," she said raising her voice.

"Go ahead," said Reggie, raising his hands in surrender.

"I didn't know how to handle the pressure and the questions people kept asking me about you guys," she said. "When you and Vinnie went to prison, it was as if my life and career simply fell apart."

"I don't get it," Reggie said abruptly. "I'm the one who went to jail. It was my fucking life that came to a screeching halt—not yours."

"I know, baby. I know," Sylvia said in a sullen tone.

Reggie was always stumped by how much confidence Sylvia exuded on the runway and in front of cameras, but how quickly she fell apart in the face of adversity. The fact that the sight of a crisis scared the shit out of her puzzled him.

"Tell me the truth," Sylvia queried, "did you think about me while you were locked down?

"No, not really," Reggie said staring into her eyes.

"Well, I can't say that I blame you. I guess seven years of marriage was enough, huh?"

"Sylvia, you wrote me, begging me for a divorce. So, I gave it to you—while I was in prison, mind you," Reggie said. Just thinking about how she couldn't wait until he got out of jail left a bitter taste in his mouth.

"Excuse me," Reggie said, rising from his seat. "But I think it's time for me to move on." He brushed past her to join Vincent, his wife Nia and some friends in a toast to his newfound freedom.

Soon, the music was turned up. Reggie couldn't stand still while George Clinton's *Flashlight* remix played at a rhythm-jolting, body-gyrating fervor. It got so hot on the dance floor between Reggie and Miss Michigan, a raven-haired beauty, that Sylvia stood up, adjusted the black lace jumpsuit she wore—sans a bra and panties—and gingerly walked over toward them.

She stood patiently behind Reggie. As soon as he performed one of his patented moves, she grabbed his wrist and spun him away from Miss Michigan. Then she took control of the dance.

"You could've asked me to dance the regular way," Reggie said, smiling and wiping the sweat off his forehead.

"I know, but I was tired of watching you and Little Miss Pageant Girl over there. She's really not your type, Reggie."

"No? Well just what is my type anyway?"

Sylvia stopped dancing, put her hands on her waist and began stroking herself down to her hips and back up to the sides of her breasts.

"Your type is quiet," she stroked downward, shaking her hips from side to side. "Unassuming," she said, stroking upward and swiveling her hips again. "She is intelligent, thoughtful, challenging, and of course, beautiful," Sylvia said punctuating each word with a provocative stroke and twist.

Reggie was mesmerized, but he caught himself staring and snapped out of it. He continued dancing with Sylvia through a variety of songs. They danced for twenty minutes or so with their bodies close for most of that time.

As the night came to a close, Sylvia offered to bed Reggie down for the night and he accepted. Reggie told her that he would rent a room for the night at a midtown hotel. Sylvia declined; telling him that she had a home upstate and that would be more conducive to their mutual interests.

Before leaving with Sylvia, Reggie excused himself to speak with Vincent. His brother handed him a tote bag containing a key to the Cottonwood, a high-rise condominium in the Riverdale section of the Bronx, a 9mm. Baretta and the keys to a dark green 1994 Nissan Altima. Reggie followed Sylvia in his new Altima to her home in Rockland County.

The road was desolate at that hour. Sylvia baited Reggie into a highway race. She wanted to show off the horsepower of her new BMW.

Once inside her home, they began to relax and Reggie asked, "Who'll close up?"

"The club?"

"Yeah, what else."

"My DJ, DeathCom. He closes for me," Sylvia answered. "The money will be deposited later this morning. Hey, you're not thinking about robbing me are you?"

"No," Reggie laughed. "I just wanna go upstairs and bless your body."

"What's that supposed to mean?" Sylvia asked coyly.

Reggie suddenly turned dead serious, "Come on now, don't play. We've come way too far for you to start acting stupid now."

Sylvia laughed—delighted that she could still push Reggie's buttons. All she had to do was promise him something then pretend to take it away. He always became livid within seconds.

Once upstairs, the mood was perfectly sexy again. Reggie was relaxed. He had a good feeling about what was about to happen. Sylvia started running the shower. Reggie turned on the television to an adult channel he found. Candles were already burning in the bathroom indicating that romance was already scheduled.

"Were you expecting someone?" Reggie asked.

"No, Baby," she stammered. "I-I know it appears that way, but that wasn't my intention."

"Really?"

"Absolutely. The candles were lit so that I wouldn't be in the dark," Sylvia replied as she began to undress.

Piece by piece, articles of clothing dropped to the bathroom floor. Reggie caught a glimpse of her glistening breasts and thighs. He was happy to be there, but couldn't help wondering about the burning candles. When Reggie and Sylvia were married burning candles indicated that she was good and horny.

"You can turn on the television if you want?" Sylvia said as she showered.

"I did," he answered.

As pulsating beads of water massaged and cascaded her finely sculpted body, Sylvia realized she wanted company.

"Reggie, come on in here with me, Baby."

Walking toward the bathroom, Reggie noticed the blurry shadow of Sylvia's naked body through the shower curtain. He tore off his clothes, entered the shower and they began to bathe each other. Minutes later, they both emerged holding hands. Reggie guided her toward the bed and then gently laid her down. Her smooth, soft, chiseled shoulders felt good to the touch. Reggie had been incarcerated for ten-plus years with hard, ugly, nasty, dirty men. He melted as Sylvia wrapped her long, shapely legs around his muscular back as they began to make love to each other.

Sylvia cooed, "Oooh, Baby...you da man. I wanted to have you first-that's all."

"What's that mean?" Reggie asked.

"Baby, you came home and I know your drippin' for it."

"I don't understand?"

"You were freakin' too hard on the dance floor with that bitch, Miss Michigan. I wasn't gonna let her leave with you."

"So that's what this is all about?" Reggie asked, loosening his embrace slightly.

"Partially, but I'm your ex-wife. You would never totally forget me, would you?"

Releasing the chimpanzee-type grip of her legs around his back, Sylvia slowly guided Reggie's fingers toward her crimson lips, placing his index finger on the tip of her tongue.

"You never forgot the technique, did you?" he asked.

She shook her head, letting him know she hadn't forgotten a thing about their love making. The former husband and wife rolled from one side of the bed to the other, building up a sexual frenzy just like old times. They knew how to open each other's doors of passion.

Beads of sweat rolled off Reggie's clean shaven face. The blue light from the television reflected on their still but panting bodies as they swayed in a synchronized rhythm. Gradually, after a three and half hour soiree, and multiple climaxes for them both, they relaxed and fell asleep wrapped in each other's arms.

The next morning, Reggie was awakened by beams of sunlight that warmed his eyes. He listened as he could make out voices coming from downstairs. He quickly dressed and went downstairs in search of Sylvia and whomever she was talking to.

As he reached the bottom of the steps, a toy car rolled passed his feet and a little girl ran to retrieve it.

"Nia, don't leave the table before you finish your breakfast," a male voice instructed.

There before Reggie's eyes was what looked like a family of four, with Sylvia included.

Inquisitive, yet soft-spoken, the little girl pondered aloud, "Who are you, Mister?"

"Nia, don't talk to strangers," the man scolded the child. "Sylvia, aren't you gonna introduce me to your friend?" the man asked.

"Everybody, this is Reggie Cochran," Sylvia said, waving her hand toward Reggie. "And, Reggie, this is my family," she added, pointing to each member. "This is my son, Ramsey; my little girl, Nia; and this is my husband, Garry."

"Ah, you're Sylvia's ex-husband, aren't you?" Garry asked.

Reggie nodded without speaking. He couldn't believe what he was seeing. He was taken aback by the impromptu breakfast party. Reggie didn't appreciate the position Sylvia delivered him into. She had remarried and kept it a secret. Her husband, had he been the type, could have blown his head off if he wanted to. She didn't give a fuck about that.

Figuring that her relationship with her husband was so shattered and open, Sylvia just brought Reggie to her home from the club with intentions of having sex with him while her family slept. She didn't care. Maybe Garry wasn't bothered by his wife's behavior. Maybe he was used to it. Reggie didn't have to find out this way. They could have gone to his place, or to a hotel or motel-anywhere but the house she shared with her husband and their kids. Talk about shitting where you sleep.

CHAPTER FIVE

Quite a Charmer

The office was no different from any other. A series of such offices stood in a row adjacent to one another across from a small waiting room filled with chairs—some of them broken—where less than noble faces awaited attention and complied with supervision.

Male and female workers scurried in and out of the rooms carrying folders or paperwork. Some occasionally stopped to check the sign-in list at the front desk to see how many people still needed to be seen.

At first glance one would assume this place to be a doctor's office or some other mundane gathering place where humans are serviced. But the difference here was that every now and then a man or woman would be led out with their hands behind their backs in a manner reminiscent of Ed Sullivan, a 1960's variety show host. Here, though, when the person walked by you noticed that they were wearing St. Louis Jewelry, a term used in the penitentiary to describe the handcuffs worn when a person is arrested or when a parolee violated the tenets of his parole agreement. This was often the case here.

It was just past 11 o'clock in the morning when Reggie arrived at the offices of the New York State Division of Parole, only about a quarter of a mile from Yankee Stadium. After leaving Sylvia's house three hours ago, he headed to the Cottenwood to shower and change before setting out to meet his parole officer for the first time.

Dressed in sweat pants, a hooded sweatshirt and a baseball cap with the words *FREEDOM* emblazed on the front, he navigated through the crowd in the building's lobby area and took the elevator up to the third floor where he checked in at the front desk.

"I'm supposed to see Ms. Landetta," Reggie informed the woman at the desk.

Ms. Landetta just happened to be walking by and quickly introduced herself before leading him to her office. Once inside, he relaxed since she didn't seem like she was out to bust his chops. As a matter of fact, she was quite attractive—about five foot six, blonde hair and the most intriguing emerald green eyes set into a thin, almond shaped face. She wore rimless eyeglasses perched atop the bridge of her small nose. Her broad shoulders allowed her fitted T-shirt to caress her breasts invitingly. Her jeans fit snug from her ankles to her waist, which harnessed her holstered firearm. Reggie thought Ms. Landetta, his parole officer, was just gorgeous. Period.

She began their meeting by informing Reggie of the parameters of his parole—the do's and don'ts that, if followed, would ensure he'd remain a free man.

"Ms. Landetta," Reggie interrupted her, "Did you study theater or drama when you were in college?"

"No, actually it was chemistry until I changed it to social work."

"You graduated?"

"Top of my class."

"I kinda figured that."

"What?"

"That you weren't a chemist."

She paused a moment, "What, I don't look like I can make the grade studying chemistry?"

"That's not it at all," Reggie said. "You see, you appear to be very intelligent—probably would have had no problem acing chemistry, but..."

"But what?"

"You're a voyager—an explorer," he continued. "You like to be on the move, preferably helping people-at least that's your intent."

Ms. Landetta smiled to indicate that he was on the right track.

"Social work...now that's your sphere of influence—where you can benefit society—which, in turn, is rewarding to yourself."

"You know, you're quite a charmer, Mr. Cochran," she said, making circles with her pen on a blank sheet of paper.

"If what you mean is that I don't want to take on any enemies and I wish to be loved by everyone, indeed I'm guilty."

"No, I mean you're quite a charmer."

"What would be the purpose of charming you? I don't have a chance in hell when it comes to influencing you," he asked.

Oh, that's not entirely accurate. Your behavior dictates how far you advance through this system."

"You take your work very seriously, don't you?" Reggie asked.

"It's my job," Ms. Landetta replied.

Reggie leaned forward, placing his forearm on his upper thigh. "Ms. Landetta," he said, "Can I ask you a personal question?"

"I don't see why not."

"Are you married?"

She paused a moment, with a purposeful smirk and replied, "No."

"It's not hard to tell."

"Oooh-kaay, now what does that mean?"

"A beautiful woman like you...independent with a great career who has her own money and carrying a gun. You're like Christy Love thawed out and shit. 'Member Christy Love?" he asked smiling at her.

"Theresa Graves, right? She was the pretty girl who was also on Rowan & Martin's Laugh-in."

"Are you old, Ms. Landetta?" Reggie asked, still leaning forward and staring deep into her green eyes, "Or do you just have an old soul?"

"Ha, probably the latter if I had to guess," She replied and averted her eyes away from his. "But anyway...are you clear on the conditions of your parole?"

"Yes I am," Reggie said, straightening up in his chair. "I am to seek and maintain employment and have no police contact."

"Good, I guess this visit is over then?"

To Reggie, P.O. Landetta appeared to be on the level and fair-the type of parole officer that wouldn't bag 'em and tag 'em to make a name for herself just to get ahead. He left her office, grateful...on many levels.

CHAPTER SIX

The Back Story

Two weeks elapsed before Reggie felt ready to leave the comfort of his 28th floor condo at the Cottenwood, a building located in the small Bronx community of Riverdale. He finally ventured out to visit friends and family in Harlem, Brooklyn and Queens before stopping at his old stomping grounds in the Soundview section of the Bronx.

When he returned home, there was a message on his answering machine. The anonymous voice on the message informed him that history would be repeating itself at 9 p.m. that night. He didn't know what to make of it. Reggie looked at his watch. It was 8:48 p.m. One thing was certain, Reggie spent the remaining twelve minutes trying to figure out what part of history was actually repeating itself. He turned on the television just in time to hear the narrative.

"To understand this intricate tale, one has to start at the beginning," the news commentator said. "It's been over eleven years since the events that have come to be known as the 'Bribe & Burn Trial' occurred..."

He couldn't believe that ATV's INSIGHT was doing a documentary about him and his brother, Vincent. Reggie felt honored, in a twisted kind of way. He decided to give Vinnie a call.

"Hey, man, they're tellin' our story in Insight right now," Reggie said. "Yeah, man, right now on channel 12."

Both brothers and what felt like the entire world watched as the story was retold.

In 1976, Vincent, a.k.a. "Vinnie", Cochran was sworn in to the New York City council, representing the 17th district in the Bronx. Vinnie became a city councilman in an unusual way.

The people of the Bronx were ready for change. So, in 1972, the 17th council district elected Joel Bernstein, a Bronx businessman with no political experience, to the seat.

Bernstein was a popular councilman, who quickly proved himself as a fast learner in New York City politics. But, in 1974, after having dinner in a Queens restaurant, Bernstein fell ill and died of a mysterious illness at his home two weeks later.

Only two days after his death, the New York Times ran an exclusive titled "Guess Who's Coming to Dinner?" which disclosed that Sean Taylor, a waiter at the restaurant who called police and emergency medical services after finding Bernstein unconscious, saw Vinnie, then a political consultant to Bernstein, leaving the restaurant just before police and EMS arrived. Police questioned Cochran, but nothing ever came of the inquiry. Nobody wanted to believe that Vinnie could have had anything to do with his mentor's death.

About a month after Joel's funeral, a special election was scheduled between Vincent Cochran and Bernstein's wife, Judy, an accomplished lawyer at a Wall Street law firm.

When the polls closed on election night, Judy Bernstein pulled out a squeaker that shook the

Bronx political community. Bernstein had garnered 52 percent of the votes to Cochran's 48 percent. The difference between the two was less than four thousand votes. Vinnie called for a recount, but later recanted his request. He didn't want to appear to be a sore loser, but by then, it was too late.

Taking out full page ads in the New York Times, the New York Post and The New York Daily News to apologize to the constituents of the 17th district, Vinnie wrote, "No one came to the aid of my doleful campaign."

Vinnie further stated that he got no support from "The Dems", which prompted him to join the Liberal Party.

Many political watchers labeled Vinnie's campaign as "primitive", adding that Vinnie took Judy for granted and had underestimated the loyalty of voters for Joel Bernstein—which was transferred to his wife, who was in her own right more than competent enough to fill his shoes.

The election had forever changed politics in the 17th district. There had never been so much mudslinging and character assassination as there was in the Bernstein-Cochran race. It polarized the community. Accusations flew back and forth. The district was clearly split in its support of either Judy or Vinnie. Those who voted for Vinnie accused the Bernstein campaign of discouraging Cochran supporters from voting. And Bernstein's supporters accused the Cochran campaign of using the same tactics.

When voters showed up at the polls they were told that they had arrived at the wrong election site. This meant they had to vote at a site on the outskirts of the district. Most people simply gave up and went home without voting at all. This amounted to between several hundred and a few thousand lost votes. The difference in this election was that few people complained. So Vinnie had no choice but to reverse his request for a recount.

The controversy would have gone on for months had it not been for a hastily scheduled joint press conference. Both Judy and Vinnie stood shoulder to shoulder, smiling at the cameras and telling the public that they had put their differences behind them. They both stated that it was more important for the city council-elect to move forward with the business of representing the district in council sessions at City Hall than for them to continue nitpicking over votes.

Judy struggled through the press conference. The last thing she wanted to do was to share the podium with Vinnie Cochran. She had heard the rumors about his involvement in the death of her husband, Joel. But she put her feelings aside for the cameras as the good of the government was what everyone expected her to represent. A display of even the slightest hostility from the Bernstein camp towards Vinnie—who had several friends in the council— could have led to filibusters by council members who were politically aligned with him.

To ensure there were no slip ups during the press conference, Judy had one of her aides distribute a flier to the press stating that "No questions would be taken after Mrs. Bernstein and Mr. Cochran made their statements."

"First," Judy said, "I want to thank everyone for braving the bad weather to be here today. The

Bronx has a history rich in political activism and must continue fulfilling this legacy through community support and civic responsibility towards meeting our common goals—which is to make the Bronx the best place in the world to live and work."

Judy had won over the press. The grieving wife who was carrying forth her late husband's dream was endearing to say the least. But the press ignored Judy's request for no questions and offered the two former rivals the chance to clear up their contention before the cameras.

"I want all my supporters to listen to me good," Vinnie instructed, pointing a stern finger at the press. "We can't move forward if we're gonna sit around and harp on past defeats."

One reporter yelled out, "So, you're trying to tell us that all this wasn't arranged—that the two of you are really fond of each other?" Sparse chuckling could be heard in the room.

"I'm sorry, but there will be no questions answered," Judy shot back.

"No, no that's one question I will answer," Vinnie interjected.

"Look, everyone knows that there is no love lost between the two of us. We're not friends, but we will co-exist together," Vinnie said.

"And with that this press conference is over," Judy said quickly. She wanted to cut off any other reporter outbursts. She turned and shook Vinnie's hand as the cameras clicked like blaring fireworks around them.

"Let me get off the stage before I puke," Vinnie whispered to one of his confidantes.

As her sleek black limousine whisked her away from the crowd of reporters, Judy silently wished her husband, Joel, could have witnessed her victory. But she quickly remembered that there would not have been a victory if Joel hadn't died while in office. Judy had no political aspirations before this time. She was comfortable as a partner in her law firm, Warner, Klass Thomason & Moore. It was one of Wall Street's best in the field of personal injury law.

She pulled down a hefty salary of $2.5 million a year at the firm. As city councilwoman, her annual salary would only be $70,000. But Judy felt strongly that it was her calling to fulfill Joel's legacy.

Judy believed that being married to Joel Bernstein for six years made her uniquely qualified to fill his shoes. When you are the woman that an elected politico comes home to, you end each day giving advice, quelling doubt and making decisions near and dear to the heart of the district.

She rested her head on the black leather seatback and smiled. *'In a couple of hours, I will be sworn in on the steps of City Hall,'* she thought to herself. But Judy had some unfinished business to attend to.

The highway sign read Mt. Moriah Jewish Cemetery Next Exit. The limo drove through the rustic gates towards lot 27. Judy took a lonely walk in the direction of Joel's grave.

"You want me to walk with you, Mrs. Bernstein?" Ronald, her chauffeur, asked.

"No, I'll be fine. I want to do this alone," she said.

As she approached Joel's grave, a tear rolled down her face. She wiped it away and began talking out loud to Joel's grave.

"You know, Joel I've always had this silly belief that we would both die of old age. I don't know why. I guess it was the love we shared. I miss you terribly. We were inseparable—until someone took you away from me, that is," she said, anger rising in her voice.

"Joel, I want to know who is responsible for this. The autopsy report was inconclusive. I refuse to believe your death was an accident," she said, wiping away the tears that were now running down her face. "Someone deliberately wanted you out of the way so that he could rise up the political ranks quickly. I wish you could scream from the grave, Joel. This despicable act cannot simply go unsolved."

Judy wept bitterly into her hands, overwhelmed by the many unanswered questions bombarding her mind.

"Mrs. Bernstein, we're gonna be late for your swearing in ceremony," Ronald said, gently putting his arm on her shoulder and leading her back to the limousine.

Meanwhile, in lower Manhattan, balloons and confetti lined the streets and steps leading to City Hall. Ten thousand people showed up in tour de force to support Judy Bernstein.

Almost everyone had heard about her story and now wanted to get a glimpse of the woman with nerves of steel. Although she arrived late-she did arrive and was subsequently sworn in before the cheering and teary-eyed crowd.

Councilwoman Bernstein was effective in her role as district advocate, holding town meetings and forums on issues ranging from rent stabilization, budget cuts and senior citizen programs to and women's issues and community policing.

She was a five foot one inch dynamo in high heels. From September 1974 to March 1975, putting in fourteen and a half hour days, six days each week, it became evident to her colleagues at the law firm that Judy Bernstein was focused on keeping her nose to the grindstone. So Judy was urged by her chief of staff, Carol Volker, to slow down or take a vacation before launching into her role as city councilwoman. Judy reluctantly agreed to a working vacation and the planning phase commenced.

During the next three weeks, a selection committee comprised of Chief of Staff Volker, Commerce Advisor William Ortiz and Bronx County Counsel Herb Littlefield listened to several proposals from the business community before approving the Bronx Seafood Import Company as sole recipient of a $2.5 million contract with the Cayman Island Seafood Export Association. The Cayman Island is rich in Blue Marlin, Yellowfin Tuna and Wahoo, a delicacy in many Bronx restaurants.

Directly preceding a press conference to announce the contract and to introduce the winning company, the New York City Medical Examiner released his final report on the death of Joel Bernstein. A lethal dose of arsenic trioxide was found in the contents of his stomach. Dr. Hughes explained that Councilman

Bernstein was fed arsenic trioxide in significant doses over an undetermined amount of time.

"What does it all mean?" Vinnie asked his lawyer, Donald Fitzroy, as they watched the press conference.

"It doesn't mean a damn thing and they know it," Fitzroy said. "So what, you were in the restaurant? So what, you left before police and EMS workers arrived at the scene? Nobody in the whole fucking establishment could say they saw you and Bernstein together. You told me you didn't do it and I believe you."

"Don, man, I didn't do it," Vinnie said, his head hanging low.

"Alright then, stop worrying about it. Now get me a beer before I charge this consult to your bill," he laughed.

Donald Fitzroy, at 257 pounds, was a jovial Texan. He once authored a diet book then expanded some 30 pounds beyond his start weight before the book's publication. His critics took him to task about that venture.

Fitzroy was an astute attorney with a flair for controversy. Even though contracts were his specialty, Fitzroy would take on a criminal case from time to time—much to the dismay of his colleagues. Typically, Fitzroy followed the same formula. He'd wait for the trial date to approach then he'd strongly advise his nervous clients to take a plea. His clients often ended up doing more time than they would have received from the trial procedure.

"I was thinking," Vinnie pondered out loud, "could suicide be the cause of Joel's death?"

"I doubt it," Fitzroy said. "Everyone knew Joel Bernstein loved life. Look, somebody killed this man. That's obvious. He was systematically fed a tasteless and odorless poison for an unknown amount of time. The media is trying to make you the silent patsy in this," Fitzroy hypothesized.

"Yeah, I know. But how come no one is looking at the wife? They lived together," Vinnie said.

"She has an alibi. She was lecturing at the University of Cincinnati at the time. Four hundred people saw her there."

Dr. Hughes concluded his report by stating that with "reasonable medical certainty" the cause of death is "highly suspicious." At that point, a final question was posed to Dr. Hughes by a reporter from The New York Post.

"Dr. Hughes," the reporter yelled. "Do you believe that Vincent Cochran is withholding information regarding the case?"

"That's not my area," Dr. Hughes said. "Investigation falls under the auspices of the N.Y.P.D.," the doctor replied before exiting the press conference. He vanished before they could bombard him with more questions. Members of the press trailed him, attempting to continue the inquiry.

"Dr. Hughes, Dr. Hughes, how 'bout one more question?" they shouted as the doctor moved quickly out of view.

Within the next two weeks, the New York Daily News reported that Cochran was on the verge of calling a press conference to "get something off his chest."

The article cited unnamed sources, but said that Cochran was seething with anger and calling rumors tying him to Joel Bernstein's death "baseless, politically motivated and designed to create adverse opinion among my supporters."

But in actuality, Vinnie Cochran had no plans to make a public statement on the matter. Acting on the advice of counsel, Vinnie maintained a low profile, shying away from fund raising events and social events alike. He even stayed away from New York Knicks home games, where he had previously been a permanent fixture.

When the media finally tracked Vinnie down, he was with his lawyer, Donald Fitzroy, leaving the offices of Random House Publishing Company, fueling suspicion that a book deal was in the works.

"Why don't you give a complete statement," a reporter asked as Vinnie and Fitzroy exited the publisher's headquarters.

"Give a complete statement to whom?" Fitzroy shouted back. "You mean depose Mr. Cochran with no trial pending or indictment imminent?" he asked. "Come on, guys. This is America. What you're asking is ridiculous."

"Who fed Joel the arsenic?" asked a female reporter.

"Neither Mr. Cochran nor I know the answer to that question," Fitzroy said. "The police are looking into that issue. Why don't you ask them?"

"Vinnie, what are you hiding?" another reporter inquired.

"Mr. Cochran has absolutely nothing to hide. But if your newspapers continue casting him in suspicion, I'm going to group you all together and slap a libel suit on you of epic proportions."

"You sure handled them," said Vinnie, grinning from ear to ear after the two men walked away from the stunned reporters.

"That's my job," Fitzroy said, breathing hard. His weight was becoming a problem. "As long as you let me do the talking," he said between breaths, "there won't be any foul ups."

"I'm scared they're gonna charge me-even though I didn't do it."

"Relax," said Fitzroy. "Things will ease up after a while. The police will find out who did this and your life will be your own again."

"You really believe that?"

"Got to, man. They're trying to create public pressure to force the District attorney's office into rushing to judgment-pushing for a grand jury indictment against you," Fitzroy explained.

"Who's doing this?"

"Good question," Fitzroy said. "I don't know. Vinnie, go home and get some rest."

"Yeah, you're probably right."

"I know I'm right," Fitzroy said. "It'll do us both a lot of good."

When Cayman Airways flight 171 landed at Owen Roberts Airport in Grand Cayman on May 9th, Councilman Bernstein exited the plane with her staff, including Volker, Littlefield and Ortiz.

Arthur Jenkins and James Rios, owners of Bronx Seafood Import Company, were also invited to take the trip for the in-person signing of the contract.

Before Judy left, she told a crowd of reporters that she would settle for nothing less than a "signature on the dotted line," referring to the contract she was taking with her.

"I know a lot of people are relying on me to deliver the goods I promised during the election," Judy explained. "I want to continue the legacy of my late husband and build on his record, because who knows how long I will serve in this capacity."

It was unusual for Judy to add that inference. No one at the time paid much attention to it.

The sheer magnitude and splendor of the Cayman Islands captivated the councilwoman's staffers. Those selected to attend the trip were delighted to have left the hustle and bustle of the streets of New York in exchange for the tranquility of this paradise.

With a tinge of cynicism, William Ortiz questioned the locals, "How do you all get any work done out here?"

"You simply bear down and get it done," spoke a mild mannered man with a Caribbean accent.

"Welcome to Grand Cayman," said Vidal Grace, the trade representative for the Cayman government who met the group at the airport. "It's my profound pleasure, and the delight of the government of Grand Cayman, to make sure your stay here is comfortable and productive."

Carol reached to pick up her bag and was stopped by Mr. Grace. "Don't be silly. We here in the

Cayman Islands intend to make your stay completely worry-free." Grace snapped his fingers and an agile driver quickly picked up Carol's bag and put the other bags into the awaiting van.

"Now, if you're ready to head to your hotel, we can be on our way," Grace said. "The ride will be very brief."

Driving through the palm tree-lined streets of Georgetown, decorated by rows of neatly manicured five story buildings left everyone at a loss for words in describing the beautiful Cayman capital.

Vidal Grace directed their attention to Seven Mile Beach. "The coastline is beautiful this time of year," he said. "You have come at a great time."

"Vidal, where are all the bums hiding?" asked Herb, who is never at a loss for words.

"Bums? What do you mean?" Vidal asked.

"I don't believe you had the nerve to ask him that, Herb," Carol said rolling her eyes.

"Be quiet, Carol. I'm talking to Vidal."

"Oh, you mean panhandlers," Vidal said. "There are none. All our citizens are well taken care of."

"Jesus Christ," Herb said. "This must be fucking Utopia. I'm going to retire and bringing my family down here. I've seen it all."

"If we don't complete this deal you might be fired by the time we get back," Carol said. Everyone in the group laughed—everyone but Judy. She was showing signs of mood swings. Judy was typically light-hearted and jovial, but all of that had changed since Joel's death.

"Tell me, Mrs. Bernstein, is there anything you want to do while you're on the island?" Vidal asked.

"I'd really like to visit a museum while I'm here," she added. "After I finish up some personal business, that is."

"Oh, come on, Judy," Herb said. "Live a little. Come scuba diving with me."

"Are you crazy? Scuba diving? Not me!" she said. "I have a responsibility to my constituency."

"Yeah, but the election is over for crying out loud," Herb said.

"Look, I'm doing a job I don't want to do," Judy said coming close to screaming at Herb. "I just lost my husband and the killer is on the loose!"

"Wait a minute. Wait a minute. What killer?" Vidal asked, holding up his hands to quiet the group.

"Well, I'm going," Carol said, ignoring Vidal's question. "I hope you change your mind, Judy. It would do you some good to have a little fun."

"Great. Have fun. Don't forget to write." Judy said, uninterested in Carol's response.

"Will someone listen to me," Vidal shouted, "What killer?"

Silence surrounded the already tranquil atmosphere. Everyone looked around to see who would explain. No one did. Vidal's request fell upon deaf ears.

"Never mind that, Vidal," said Carol.

"How long before we're at the Hyatt?"

Judy and her staffers had endured enough quizzing in the U.S. so it was easy for them to blow off Vidal's direct question.

"Your timing is impeccable," Vidal said. "We have arrived."

"Wow. This is breathtaking," William said.

The Hyatt Regency Grand Cayman is a 235 room alcazar of all you want and need in luxurious accommodations. Pleasantly smiling hotel workers were never too far from the beck and call of guests. Each room featured marble entrances, an oversized bathtub, fully stocked bar and French-style doors. For $2,000 more, well-endowed guests enjoyed rooms with verandas and monogrammed bathrobes.

Tired, ready to relax and wind down, Judy, Carol, Herb, Arthur, and James checked into their perspective rooms to retire for the night.

The junket began the next morning with a breakfast meeting in the main banquet hall of the hotel. The elaborate event was designed to introduce all the players to each other and was hosted by the Cayman's Governor.

Following breakfast, William, James, Arthur and Vidal met in an elegant conference room located below ground level to begin hammering out the particulars of the contract. Within three hours, a final product was agreed upon worthy of the following day's contract signing. Once Vidal explained the Grand Cayman's liberal tax laws and incentives afforded foreign companies, James and Arthur were fully aware that no other venture between two entities would fare more lucrative.

In an attempt to fill Judy in on the good news, William called her room from a phone in the lobby. It rang endlessly, so he left a message for her at the hotel desk.

"Can you make sure Mrs. Bernstein gets this message?" he asked the receptionist. "It's urgent."

"Yes sir," said the hotel worker.

On the other side of the island, off Frank Sound, Carol and Herb were scuba diving with several tourists in the Cayman's crystal blue waters. They nibbled on stuffed lobster with wheat crackers between dives. Carol fell in love with the archaic scenery, which told of a peaceful and mysterious underwater world.

Later that evening in the lobby of the Hyatt, William grew more concerned over the whereabouts of Councilwoman Bernstein. *'Where could she be?'* he wondered.

Several messages left at the front desk had gone unanswered. *'Could she have met some handsome Cayman native and run off with him? After all, she was single now,'* William thought.

He had noticed that Judy had cut her hair and dyed it a warm auburn. It might not have amounted to much, but William had been through two divorces. His last had him observing his ex-wife's coming out party. Toni, his now-ex-wife, had let her hair grow, started wearing skirts above the knee and began aggressively chasing men. William knew from experience that women typically treated themselves to a makeover before starting over.

Just prior to the Cayman trip, William asked Judy when she was going to begin dating again. Months had passed since Joel's death and William felt she deserved a new beginning. But Judy was old fashioned. She felt she shouldn't rush into a dating relationship so soon. Now, with her missing, William would have given anything for Judy to appear.

"Whew! Boy that was long day," William heard a voice saying from a distance.

Carol Volker and Herb Littlefield had returned with several tourists from their scuba diving excursion.

"Well, if it isn't Stubby and Lord Albert," William said, greeting them.

"Who in the hell are you calling Stubby?" Carol asked. "My legs may be short and chunky, but I don't have to be reminded of it."

"For someone just returning from a good time, you sure are bitchy," William said.

"Look, it's not my fault you couldn't go scuba diving with us," Carol replied. "Judy brought you along specifically because you work well with the business community. We all have work to do and we've been doing it," she added.

"When were you working? William asked sarcastically. "In between dives?"

"Now that's low, William," Herb said. "What are you doing here in the lobby? Did Judy send you down here to make us feel bad when we got back?"

"No," William said.

"Where is Judy anyway?" Herb asked.

"I thought she was with you guys. I haven't seen her since breakfast," William answered.

As soon as the breakfast meeting ended, everyone rushed off in separate directions to enjoy the island. No one knew where the councilwoman was and no one seemed to care until now.

Carol was reluctant to alert the Cayman authorities of Judy's disappearance. She didn't want to embarrass Judy—especially if she was only off taking some time to be by herself. But it was Carol's job to be aware of Mrs. Bernstein's whereabouts at all times. She realized that she had goofed off, going scuba diving and not once considering Judy. Once she and Herb left the hotel for Franks Sound she simply forgot her obligation.

Sensing a need to safeguard their privacy, Carol, Herb and William moved their conversation to a nearby gazebo outside the hotel's lobby. Herb suggested they establish auxiliary plans in case the councilwoman failed to return. He insisted phone calls be made to the U.S. to alert the council president and the mayor of the predicament. First, though, they all agreed that someone had to check Judy's room for any clues that would explain her whereabouts.

Upon entering Mrs. Bernstein's room with the help of housekeeping, William noticed everything inside seemed to be in order. The bed was still unmade. Papers were stacked on a table near the window—nothing unusual there. He noticed drafts of a speech Judy had been preparing to make after the contract was signed tomorrow. He went into the bathroom and turned the faucet off. A steady stream of water had been running as if Judy forgot to turn it all the way off. Still, there was nothing unusual about the room.

"Will that be all, sir?" inquired the chambermaid.

"Yes, thank you. And this is for you," he said, handing her a generous tip. The maid left, but William walked back into the room after noticing a piece of paper next to the lamp on the nightstand. The note read, Silver Sands—Noon. William didn't know what to make of it. He put it back and turned to leave the room.

"What are you looking for?" Judy said, standing in the doorway.

"Oh, I know how this must look, Judy, but we hadn't seen you all day," William said. "I was sent up here to see if I could find out where you had gone. The contract is ready and Herb needs you to look it over before morning," he rambled on.

"William Ortiz, this is my room," Judy shouted. "How dare you search my room? I'm surprised at you."

The clamor between Judy and William drew Carol and Herb from their rooms. They were astonished at the councilwoman's appearance. Always the picture of vibrancy, Judy now appeared tired and worn down. Her powder blue slacks were wrinkled and her blouse was only tucked in on one side. No one had the nerve to ask Mrs. Bernstein what happened or where she'd been.

"Hey, you guys," Herb said. "What's going on here?" Herb positioned himself between William and Judy, who were nose to nose.

"I came back to my room to find this asshole snooping around, looking for God knows what," Judy said.

Carol stood back and allowed Herb to do all the talking. He was doing a good job so far.

"I sent him up here to see if you were in the room," Herb said. "We have to look over the contract, Judy. I take full responsibility for my decision, okay?"

"Go get the damn contract, William," Judy said.

While William went back to his room to fetch the contract, Carol and Herb noticed that she was mumbling to herself. That was unusual for Judy, but no one said a word to her.

"I like William-I really do, but I won't stand for no fucking snooping," Judy shouted, her hands grasping her hips, "Problems, I got 'em up to here," she yelled, raising her right hand above her head to indicate the height of her problems. "Believe me when I say it. You think I'm overreacting? Well, think again. I'm completely justified."

Herb and Carol found it hard to understand Judy's behavior. They never witnessed her acting this way.

"You think I'm crazy, right? But I'm not," Judy said as she took a seat beside the bed. "I've really had a rough day, excuse me."

Carol could no longer be silent, "Oh, no we don't think you're crazy, Judy. You're just under a considerable amount of stress."

Staring at the two of them like she was fully aware of their intentions, Judy answered, "Yeah, well why do you two keep staring at me like that?"

"Like what?" Herb and Carol replied harmoniously.

"Like I stole something. Don't look at me like that, please." Straightening her clothing, Judy felt better now that she got that off her chest.

"I know you're the boss, Judy and I shouldn't ask you this..." Carol said.

"What?"

"Is someone after you? I mean are you in trouble or something?"

Judy waited a second or two, surprised by the question, and then replied, "William put you up to this, didn't he? It was William, right?"

Carol told Judy she was absolutely wrong about this. She insisted to Judy her question was based on her own personal observation-her own curious mind at work.

By the time William returned with the contract, Judy had calmed down enough for the three of them to discuss the details. Judy decided to let Arthur and James remain in their rooms until morning.

"I don't need Arthur and James to see me in this condition," she said. "Let them sleep."

The contract meeting went on for two hours. The foursome also discussed the rally for the homeless in City Hall Park, council meetings on education, a pay raise for council members, the Mayor's State of the City Address and Judy's upcoming speech at the Bronx Latin Business Association Luncheon.

Carol remembered to mentioned that last night; Deputy Mayor Fisk called to make it known to that Molly's Diner, the infamous "kitchen of death", where Joel Bernstein had his last bowl of Chili Con Carne, was shut down until further notice.

Carol could call to mind the countless hours Judy spent galvanizing sympathizers in civilized protest to shut down Molly's Diner. On one occasion, as tension started to flare, a police officer was struck in the head with a large rock and hospitalized for three days. Judy felt gratified to know that her prayers had been answered. The public wouldn't allow Joel's death to be forgotten.

As William, Carol and Herb left the councilwomen's room to turn in for the night, Judy felt compelled to apologize for her behavior earlier. They all accepted her offering immediately.

In the hallway, no one was more thrilled with the way this episode turned out than William. He was ecstatic, and well he should be, considering the fact that he could have had hell to pay had he been caught red handed with that note.

Despite the condition she was in last night, Judy was able to take her place behind Bronx Import Company owners, Arthur Jackson and James Rios, for the contract signing that took place at the Cayman Islands National Museum.

The "invitation only" ceremony was attended by 150 of the island's elite, who were treated to smoked turkey loin, corn burgundy and wild rice before having the privilege of listening to the councilwoman's glad-to-be-doing-business-with-you speech. She received hearty praise for her initiative to make the first fishing export contract between a Bronx small business and the Cayman Islands a reality. If Judy could've run for office in the Caymans, "she would win easily," a native Caymanian present at the ceremony revealed.

Later that evening, back in New York, Vinnie and Nia were entertaining guests when Donald Fitzroy called.

"I got bad news. Judy Bernstein was found dead in her hotel room in the Cayman Islands," Donald said in an anxious tone.

"Oh my God," Vinnie said. "What happened?"

"When she didn't show up for her flight back to New York, hotel security broke into her room and found her, apparently beaten to death."

Vinnie held the phone to his ear but couldn't hear anything after Donald relayed the crushing news.

"Are you there, Vinnie?" Donald asked, noticing the lull in conversation.

"Yeah. Yeah, I'm still here."

"Well, at least now you won't have to worry about the D.A. trying to stick you with this murder."

"How come?" Vinnie asked.

"Because you weren't in the Caymans earlier this afternoon and-"

"That's all?" Vinnie interrupted Donald. "That don't mean shit. You have to come up with something better than that."

Donald paused a moment, "How 'bout you're gonna be councilman soon...how's that?"

"Come on. Stop pulling my leg for Christ's sake."

"No, I'm serious. I never lie about your future, you know that. But pursuant to election law EL 220.4 (a), "In the event that the mechanics of local government cease and desist, leaving a specific group or constituents without leadership or representation for a period of time that shall not exceed two calendar years, the candidate with the second highest computation of votes must be installed." This stature is called election special circumstance and it's just that, special."

The phone dropped. Donald could hear Vinnie rejoicing with Nia in the background, "Holy shit, I'm gonna be councilman, babe."

"Well, not just yet," Donald said when Vinnie returned to the phone. Several procedural steps have to play out before Vinnie could take his seat in the Council.

"Nia wants to know when we can move in?" Vinnie asked, ignoring his lawyer's last statement.

"Oh boy," Donald said to himself. He knew he had to meet with Vinnie to explain the law and slow him down.

If Vinnie didn't believe that indeed a tragedy did occur, then the headline in the New York Times the next morning clarified things. It read: NYC POL BEATEN TO DEATH IN CARIBBEAN. The article went on to tell New Yorkers that Judy Bernstein had been found dead in her Cayman Island hotel room. The newspaper further reported that when the councilwoman failed to show up at the airport for a 7:15 a.m. return flight to New York, Carol Volker, her chief of staff, grew concerned. Once the councilwoman didn't answer her telephone or repeated knocks at the door, hotel authorities were called. Upon entering the room, they found her body in a pool of blood.

Bernstein's skull was crushed and her body badly beaten. She had been raped repeatedly and the killer shredded her panties. Just in case her murder wasn't gruesome enough, her vagina was ripped from her body. A search for that body part was ongoing.

A detective on the island present at the crime scene told the Cayman Compass newspaper that "This here case has organized crime written all over it." He also explained that the island has a peace manifest. "People here don't execute others," he said. "It's usually outsiders who commit such acts."

In the days succeeding the murder, shock and sadness overwhelmed the Bronx district Judy represented. No one could believe she died so soon after her husband. Constituents attached pink and white ribbons to the trees outside their homes in remembrance of their fallen leader. However, the 17th district was no closer to filling that vacant seat for the second time in almost two years because the city council president has to declare Judy's seat vacant and reopen it. And papers needed to be filed with the Board of Elections by the runner-up, in this case, Vincent Cochran, to inform them that he either would or wouldn't accept the vacancy. The process was slow moving, with hearings on the matter held six months after filing. It wouldn't be until July before this issue could be dealt with. Plus a formal decision in writing would take at least another six months.

The following month, Vincent ignored his lawyer's advice to lay low and instead emerged from a political cocoon-attempting to salvage a dream and fulfill a commitment. He went on a whirlwind tour, visiting city council members and sitting in on hearings. In the Parkchester section of the Bronx, Vinnie sang with the children at the Wee Lo Day Care Center and accepted an invitation to field questions from callers on a morning talk show.

In July, the hearings on *Election Special Circumstance* got under way without incident. Mr.

Fitzroy had an extended conversation with his client, telling Vinnie that this was a sensitive time and that there should be no more appearances for a while. By hearing's end, the way was paved for Vinnie to take the infamous seat.

The investigation into Judy Bernstein's murder took a positive turn when it was learned that Caymanian police had called Lana Dixon, a woman who told police she was present in the lobby of the Hyatt Regency Grand Cayman and witnessed a man running from the hotel about the time law enforcement officials alleged the murder took place.

Details were sketchy, but on a rainy, foggy May afternoon, Customs officials at Roberts Owen Airport detained a man attempting to board a plane with what they described as a "suspicious content."

That "content", wrapped in ice inside a picnic cooler was later identified by Caymanian police as a body part. It was then that the police began to wonder if this body part belonged to the murdered councilwoman.

Police arranged for the body part to be hauled off for positive analysis. Those tests determined the body part to be a human vagina. The suspect was subsequently arrested on the charge of suspicion of tampering with physical evidence.

At the time, there was practically no link between the suspect and the murder. Until the suspect, unaware that his calls were being monitored at the island jail, made a call to North Carolina that was traced to the home of Ernie "Flash" Resnick, the reputed king of the numbers racket on Tobacco Road.

When confronted with the information, he denied it. But when the tape of the jailhouse phone conversation was played back, the suspect broke down and admitted the whole scheme. The suspect, Roy Wendell, revealed that he was hired to kill Judy Bernstein by Ernie Resnick.

New York City police, aware of the Wendell confession, were now entertaining the notion that Wendell might have killed Joel Bernstein too. Wendell told police that he never met Joel and that the only time he ever saw the late- councilman was in the newspapers. But he offered them his theory on Joel's murder—saying that Judy, tired of paying off Joel's gambling debts, had "iced" Joel herself.

Police were impressed. They were beginning to believe that Roy Wendell's theory was plausible, so they wanted to hear more. Wendell said that Joel owed more money than he could ever pay back. That's the way Resnick wanted it. He pressured Joel to pressure Judy to have sex with him to pay off the debt. She reluctantly agreed. But no matter how many times she had sex with him; Resnick always said that "this time" was the last time. It never was.

So one day Judy got an idea—a final solution type of idea. She poisoned Joel slowly until he died that day in the restaurant. Judy figured this horrible episode would be over, instead, it got worse.

When Resnick heard that Judy was going to be in the Caymans, he flew down to the Caribbean island and settled into the Silver Sands Hotel. After several attempts, he finally reached Judy by phone. She said she would come over, but by the next day, she was dead. Wendell said he followed Judy from the Silver Sands back to the Hyatt, but too many people were present in the hallway to her room. So he waited until the following day. As Judy prepared to leave her hotel room for the airport, he pushed his way in and in his own words, "did the job."

The pie-faced Wendell, dressed in a brown sweat suit and tennis shoes, spoke slowly with the passion of a Bible salesman, making sure that his words were understood.

Then police asked him if all he had to do was kill Judy Bernstein, why did he cut out her vagina? Roy told investigators that might be enough for some clients, but not Resnick. He wanted proof, Roy said. "I got it for him."

Now caught, Wendell's confession was an attempt to preserve his life, if not his freedom. Furthermore, he could never live comfortably after fingering Resnick, who killed traitors, or anyone for that matter, without malice.

Caymanian police informed the NYPD that after the investigation was complete Roy Wendell would be charged and tried for the murder and sexual mutilation of Judy Bernstein. Conviction meant immediate death by hanging, making it virtually impossible for Wendell to cooperate with their investigation.

NYC police were disappointed that the opportunity to interview Wendell would not be forthcoming. Nevertheless, their search of the Bernstein home did uncover arsenic trioxide in a cabinet under the kitchen sink.

Police never figured Judy to be a suspect because she was out of town lecturing at the University of Cincinnati.

By accident a rookie police officer present at the crime scene noticed a crystallized substance on the counter top near the sugar bowl. His curiosity allowed him to taste it. He told his superiors that the sugar wasn't sweet.

The sugar, along with several other items, was removed from the Bernstein home and taken to the police laboratory for analysis. When the results came back positive for arsenic trioxide, police investigators were firmly convinced that Joel Bernstein met his death at the hands of his wife, Judy.

Donald Fitzroy was livid when he finally caught up with Vincent at a local Bronx tavern, thrashing open the front door so that a booming noise emitted and frightening patrons. "What the hell are you doing? I told you to lay low and what do you do? You casually visit a day care center, but you don't stop there, you also drop in on a morning talk show. You just don't give a fuck, do you?"

"Come on, Don..."

"Come on Don," the attorney said, mocking Vincent, "You're ruining everything before you get anything."

Without looking in Donald's eyes Vincent replied, "I thought you said the damn council seat was mine?"

"It is."

"Well then, I'm merely reaching out to my people. That's all. The people I'll soon represent. Is that a crime?"

"They're not your people yet." Donald emphasized as he seated himself besides Vincent. "The process has to run its course."

Every time Donald gave Vincent advice, Vincent became more convinced that Donald liked to hear himself speak. He would go on and on about "the right way to do this or that."

Resting his head against his right hand, Vinnie turned towards Donald-looking him straight in his eyes and said, "When I get that seat I want you on board. I want you to be a part of the team."

"That's generous of you Vinnie, but I can't accept," Donald retorted-bowing out gracefully, "I think I'm more valuable to you outside of the council. Besides, I don't know shit about politics. You'll find someone who'll suit you and your agenda. You'll see."

"I hardly know shit either," Vincent rebutted, "If it was up to knowledge, two thirds of the people who serve wouldn't do it. But that's beside the point. I respect your decision. If you feel that you can't work with me in good faith I understand."

Vincent turned and gestured towards the bartender and said, "Two beers please."

With an earnest expression on his face the bartender said, "Didn't I tell you about sitting on my stools, Don? You're too damn fat. I told you that didn't I?"

"Fuck you!" Don shot back. "That's why you're a bartender you stupid motherfucker. Vinnie, I'll be in touch," he said and turned to leave.

Watching Donald's oval-shaped body storm out of the tavern prompted a chuckle from the bartender and Vincent.

January 6, 1976 will be remembered for two reasons: The New York Knicks return to Madison Square Garden after a grueling 11 game, 14 day road trip. And it was also the day Vincent Cochran was belatedly sworn in as a New York City Councilman.

A party was held at the Harvard Hilton, a luxurious fifty two story hotel located near the Hutchinson River Parkway, a major thoroughfare.

New York City politicians gravitated toward the new energy Vinnie brought. Most showed up because they thought Vinnie would be an important player in the implementation of a variety of agendas in their district. Others showed up to be seen. And others simply came for the free food.

Eleven hundred invites flocked to the "Bronx Taj Mahal" to celebrate with the recipient of a council seat resulting from *Election Special Circumstance.* Hundreds of red, white and blue balloons were released from the ceiling as the newly-sworn city councilman and his wife approached the podium.

Following a short speech, Vinnie left the stage to return to his table. On his way down the aisle, he was stopped by an elderly woman who asked, "How does it fell to be a Bronx councilman?"

Suddenly Vincent understood the power of the position he just undertook. He noticed the phony smiles on people's face as they performed deeds worthy of a monarch.

"You want some friendly advice?" the elderly woman continued, "Don't let the job consume you. I've seen many men and women corrupted by the power. Don't become a victim."

"I'll keep that in mind, ma'am," Vinnie said, wondering just how much acumen that woman had.

"Did we meet in Bora Bora?" a perky brunette asked. She resembled a television actress from the 1960s. Vincent said they hadn't, but continued to listen to the woman.

"I've been there twice you know and it was boring. It gets boring after the first visit, actually," the woman said.

"Really, that's interesting," Vinnie paused for a second, "I hope you don't mind, I'm wanted on the other side of the room."

"Who's that?" Nia inquired walking towards Vincent.

"No one. I never saw her before in my life."

When Vinnie and Nia returned to their table, a bottle of champagne sat beside a note which read: Congratulations. Live up to your power. The note was signed with the initials D.M.

"Who left this bottle on my table?" Vincent asked.

"That plump gentleman sitting between those two men over there," the waiter answered.

"Do you know him, Vincent?" Nia asked. Vincent told his wife that he had never met that gentleman, but would accept the bottle out of respect.

Walking away, the waiter stopped in his tracks as if remembering something he had to say, "Oh, yes. Your brother left a message."

"What did he say?"

"That he would be late. His plane was delayed."

"I don't believe this. He already missed the swearing in ceremony. Now who knows when he'll get here."

Several minutes later, a taxi pulled up in front of the hotel. Reggie had finally arrived-late but present. He couldn't wait to exalt his brother for making good on a childhood dream. While Reggie was running the streets hustling basketball games, Vincent was obtaining a bachelor's degree in Political Science from New York University.

Vincent's offer of the position of Director of Travel and Recreation was unforeseen by Reggie, who found himself on the verge of looking for a real job.

"Look, I'm not gonna sit here and beat on you about being late. You're here and that's what counts," Vinnie said to his brother when they hugged.

"I'm here because you asked me to. You don't have to worry about me embarrassing you, Vinnie."

"I'm not, but you need to be candid with me. Is there anything I should know about your past before it pops up?"

"No. Nothing I can think of."

"You sure?"

"Yeah. Shit, what is this, an inquisition? I said no and I mean no!"

"Okay. Good." Vinnie retorted, leaning closer to Reggie so as to reduce the distance between the two of them. "You see this is New York City government. And if the shit ain't right out there in the open it becomes a cancer that slowly eats its way through your term. You weren't here, but I had to endure a lot of adversity to get this seat. Nia will tell you-she's been my rock throughout this ordeal."

With passion he continued to express his internal feelings about the Bernstein murders and how public sentiment shifted between love and hate until the murders were solved.

Reggie was astonished to hear about the turmoil Vinnie endured over the past two years. He felt a bit angered that Vinnie hadn't confided in him, his own brother, when he could've used his support most.

"My head was swirling from all the controversy-you don't know. Besides, you were so far away in North Carolina."

"What? You couldn't use the telephone. You didn't have arthritis in your fingers when you called me to New York for the swearing in. What's the difference?"

Vincent couldn't answer his brother. He knew his brother was right. Reggie wouldn't stand by and let the press and the District attorney's office blacken Vincent's name and reputation.

"Hey, I'm not gonna sit here and beat on you about that. You say it's over, then it's over. I don't know much about this political stuff, but I do know one thing . . .

"What?"

"I won't stand by in the future and let forces with petty personal interests destroy everything you worked so hard for."

"What are you talking about?"

"Come on, Vincent you know this is politics and they push people around. Only this time you've got security," Reggie said resoundingly sure of his commitment to stand by Vincent if and when times get lean.

The next morning, in his official capacity as a city councilman, Vincent sauntered into his new City Hall office accompanied by his brother only to find someone waiting for him.

"I know you didn't expect a visitor this early in the morning, but I wanted to catch you before you began your day." Mayor Peterson said, spinning around to reveal himself.

"I just hope I can count on you for support in the council. If we act together, we'll stand a chance against the Republicans. They can't get a damn thing done in the State Assembly. In City Hall we'll try to avoid the same stalemate."

"I'd love to help in any way I can if my district can benefit from my involvement," Vincent declared.

"Good," said Mayor Peterson.

"Have you met my brother, Reggie?" Vincent said.

Reaching out to shake Reggie's hand, Mayor Patterson said, "Pleased to meet you. Look, I have a meeting to attend, but I had to see you first. Stop by sometime-my office is down the hall."

"I will." Vinnie pledged walking towards his desk as the mayor left the office.

"I don't understand," he said scratching his head muttering, "Mayor Patterson never uttered anything positive about me during the election."

"If I were you, Vincent, I wouldn't trust him with both eyes open and a flashlight."

Councilman Cochran became a member of the Committee on Land Use, where community and commercial development are regulated. Vincent received several visitors interested in swaying his opinion. An appearance at the New York Coliseum for the opening of Home Expo '76 proved to change the course of many lives to come, especially after Councilman Cochran met David Markoff, founder of Markoff Home Builders, leaders in affordable housing for more than 27 years.

Even though Vincent wasn't sure if he should associate with Markoff, he wasn't about to be disparaging. They exchanged words-then David handed Vincent a business card with a telephone number written above where a scratched out number previously appeared.

"Call me, please." The dark-suited developer requested as he walked away from Vincent.

That night after Vincent returned home, he prepared to shower. As he removed his pants, his wallet fell from his back pocket. From that pocket a business card slid out and fell to the carpet. Vinnie picked it up and immediately remembered where he knew Markoff from. It was at the Harvard Hilton on the night of the swearing in party. The champagne on the table—the man sitting between those two gentlemen was D.M., David Markoff.

Efforts by Markoff to reach the councilman in an appeal to obtain a waiver from the Board of Estimate, using the councilman as a functionary, had been fruitless. Aides notified Vincent of his district's renewed interest in the now-defunct Hugo View project and a building tycoon's attempt to circumvent city contract protocol.

Hugo View was the creation of two Brooklyn developers who envisioned six 7-story buildings designed to resemble a European village that three hundred and fifty homeless citizens would call home. This project was hatched several years prior, when then-councilman; Joel Bernstein was looking for a public project he could lend his support to. As a consultant to Bernstein, it was Vincent Cochran's job to search for a project that could be developed in his Bronx district.

When builders wouldn't agree to re-locate Hugo View to the Bronx, the project fell by the waist side. It was rumored that private investment wasn't forthcoming. However, an unanticipated surge in the homeless population prompted the City Council to vote $10 million of the city budget be allocated to fund Hugo View under one condition—that Hugo View be built and managed by economically, disadvantaged minority small businesses.

David Markoff had his lawyers search for a way around the law that would make it possible for his company to build Hugo View. With a grand model of the project perched on a table within view, Markoff, according to friends, was fed up. He summoned his loyalists to his office for a strategy meeting.

"David, I have some bad news for you. You won't be able to get the Hugo View project," one aide said.

"Why? What's wrong?"

"It turns out that the Hugo View is a minority project, set aside for economically, disadvantaged small businesses. I'm sorry, David you're financially over-qualified."

"That's bullshit! I'm gonna get that contract one way or the other."

"How?" Another aide asked.

"That's your job," Markoff said, pointing to his aide, Cedric. "That's why you get paid the big bucks around here—to settle glitches like this."

"Glitch? This ain't no glitch, David.

It's the law," Cedric said.

"I know, but you're gonna get me around all that Cedric. I know you are," David said smiling.

That's when Cedric's face turned abruptly somber. "I-I-I figured you would say that."

Cedric handed Markoff a piece of paper.

"What's this," Markoff said, looking at the paper.

"It's my resignation, effective immediately." Cedric said.

The others in room sat back astonished-looking at each other

"I'm sorry, David, but I can't be part of this. I have a family to think about.

"David Markoff's face tightened. His eyes narrowed to a squint.

"So this is how you show your gratitude-after all I've done for you? It's remarkable how a people forget. When you had those parking tickets worth $2,000.00, who took care of it for you?"

"You did," Cedric responded keeping his head down.

At six-foot, two inches tall, David Markoff was used to talking down to people.

"And who gave you time off when you had those quote-unquote "personal problems?"

"You did."

"That's okay. You know, it's better to find out the limits of one's loyalty before the showdown. I'll just cut my losses now, rather than lose my shirt later."

Prosecutors in the Cayman Islands worked swiftly to procure an arrest warrant for Ernie "Flash" Resnick. Cayman homicide investigators boarded a plane armed with an arrest warrant and the pre-arranged cooperation of the North Carolina Police Department.

Relying on information contained in Roy Wendell's affidavit to the court, a joint group of investigators converged on Resnick's Cape Hatteras beach home in an effort to arrest him. He eluded them within minutes of their arrival. Between not wanting to take the rap and a phobia for detention, Ernie "Flash" Resnick became a fugitive.

One investigator said that Resnick, based on Wendell's affidavit, was reeking with guilt. In it, Wendell remembers "Flash" grabbing $70,000.00 from a dresser drawer and placing it in his hands with the instructions: "Before you kill Judy Bernstein, I want her badly beaten and when you finish, bring me a souvenir."

As lawmen closed in on Resnick, "Flash" was held up in an abandoned railroad factory about ten miles from his beach home. Residents were drawn to the railroad factory after hearing two shots fired from that direction.

Soon after people in the town discovered where the shots came from, they became witnesses to the shot a barefooted Resnick fired under his chin, thus committing suicide in front of an audience.

Chief of Staff, Charles Fuller, at a planning meeting informed Councilman Vinnie Cochran that lawyers for Roy Wendell might entertain the possibility of calling his brother, Reggie, as a witness at his upcoming trial.

Fuller explained that Reggie's appearance in a North Carolina courtroom would renew the public's view that the councilman, in one way or the other, was involved in the Bernstein murders.

"I know, I should have told you I was on Wendell's witness list," Reggie said to Vinnie, "but I didn't want you to worry prematurely."

Reggie explained to his brother that not only did he work for Resnick, but that they were friends. Reggie said that he was also present and an unwilling participant during many planning sessions for Judy Bernstein's murder.

In the beginning, Reggie believed that the murder of Judy Bernstein would go unsolved, but all that changed in a Grand Cayman Airport with the capture of Roy Wendell, who told authorities that Judy's murder was Resnick's idea.

Reggie reassured Vincent that he had nothing to do with the planning or the actual murder. Moreover, Reggie began to believe that it was time for a change of occupation.

All Reggie and Vincent could do was wait and pray that Wendell's attorney didn't need Reggie's testimony. And above all things, they hoped that Reggie's affiliation to Resnick was never made public.

In the months ahead, Vincent began to feel more comfortable about his council position and filled his days greeting visitors, attending meetings and hosting fund raising events for re-election. He also made occasional speeches to various political groups.

When Vinnie met with David Markoff, he made his feelings known that there would be no exceptions to the rule. He then suggested to Markoff that he not stand in the way of Hugo View. In that instant, David Markoff set out to make Councilman Cochran regret that decision.

Through highly placed friends in the FDIC, Markoff was able to obtain the councilman's personal savings account number. With that number, he wired $100,000.00 into that account.

When the money cleared, copies of the serial numbers, along with Markoff's own personal markings as proof, were sent to the Bronx District attorney's office, via certified mail with a cover letter informing the D.A. of Councilman Cochran's acceptance of a bribe in return for a special waiver that would allow Markoff Home Builders to receive the contract to build Hugo View. That evidence was enough for the district attorney to issue an arrest warrant for Councilman Cochran.

Three days before Markoff and Vincent met; David was saying to friends that if he didn't receive a favorable resolution, the Councilman would, in Markoff's own words, "Have problems."

Vinnie was on the phone accepting a constituent's appreciation for straightening out a social security snafu, when police marched into his City Hall office and placed him under arrest for accepting a bribe.

He was led out in handcuffs in front of his staff and only a stone's throw away from Mayor Patterson's office. Vincent was ashamed of the theater his arrest had produced.

At his arraignment on March 19, 1977 in Bronx Criminal Court, Vinnie pleaded "Not guilty" before Judge Thomas Keegan, who set bail at $20,000.00.

Reggie was out of town arranging for an upcoming fact-finding trip when he learned of Vincent's arrest. He cut his stay short to fly home and bail his brother out.

"I think I'm being set up," Vinnie whispered into the phone to Reggie.

"By who?"

"I'm not sure. My spies have their eyes and ears open though."

"You better check out the people you do business with. I don't know much about politics, but someone's trying to send you a message."

"Yeah, what message?"

"They don't like your politics," Reggie said.

For several days, headlines about the councilman's alleged acceptance of a bribe dominated the newspapers. On Monday the front page news said: Bronx Councilman Arrested. On Wednesday, the headline read: Bronx Pol Dragged Out of City Hall in Handcuffs. And Friday's paper read: Councilman Cochran Arrested and Disgraced.

Vincent Cochran had endured being the target of suspicion during the aftermath of Joel Bernstein's death. Even to get elected-he had to break through complex political barriers designed to discourage individuals from seeking public office. In a last ditch effort to destroy what credibility Councilman Cochran had left, he was being taken to the wall by unknown individuals who played rough, really rough.

Eager to get the first exclusive interview, reporters from news agencies left countless messages at the councilman's home. Vincent refused comment, although he did release a statement to the press that read, "Attempts to vilify me with scurrilous charges do no good for anyone-but they do further the consolidation of contrary political ideas."

Vinnie soon realized that his colleagues and constituents were beginning to treat him like a person with an infectious disease. His twice a week working lunches with Councilman Louis Rinali(D-Brooklyn) were now defunct and a bipartisan group of councilmen and women stated publically that they would put through a resolution barring Vincent from all city council responsibilities until his name is cleared.

Lying in bed late one night, Nia noticed Vincent staring up at the ceiling. She rolled over and rubbed his hairy chest.

"So, what are you gonna do?"

"I don't know. My colleagues in the council suggested that I step aside until this issue is rectified."

"What did you tell them?"

"I told them, hell no! " he snapped. "You know how hard I worked to get this seat. Donald will get me out of this."

Nia shook her head. She didn't have much confidence in Donald's ability to restore her husband's favorable rating with the voters. An election year beckoned on the horizon and Nia was worried about Vincent's chances.

"Are you going ahead with the fund raiser next week?"

"Of course," Vincent said, "the invitations were already sent out. Besides, what would the people who support me say if I cancelled now? It would look like an admission of guilt."

"I guess you're right, Babe."

"I know I'm right," Vincent said, turning to look his wife directly in her eyes. "Please, Nia, I've got too many things working against me at the moment. Don't you turn on me, too."

"I'm not turning on you, Vinnie."

"You're trying to confuse me."

"How am I trying to confuse you?"

"Your body language speaks volumes. It shows the lack of confidence you have in Don and I don't need that from you."

Nia noticed how the strain of the charges he was facing was taking its toll on her husband. Lately, petty skirmishes easily turned into full-scale arguments. And while she had her reservations about Donald Fitzroy she was grateful that he was able to postpone the case until the end of the councilman's term, expiring in 1980.

In the spring of 1978, Assistant District attorney Mario Carluchi submitted and received an order to show cause as to why the People v. Cochran should be given a trial date forthwith. In an order to show cause, the D.A. has to argue why the presiding judge should reverse his decision and set a trial date.

At the hearing on May 26th, held in Part 48 of Bronx Supreme Court before Judge Earl Lassiter, ADA Carluchi submitted a 35-page affidavit, signed by the state's primary witness, who had remained a mystery until now. In the affidavit the witness states that he did what any red-blooded American would do if they had information that Councilman Cochran was corrupt. Acting on that information, the confidential witness set out to see how enterprising Vincent Cochran really was. Using a community development project, the witness let it be known in the business community that his company was willing to pay handsomely for the opportunity to procure the venture.

Enter Councilman Cochran, who approached the witness and explained that, "If there is gonna be a deal, and I'm not saying that there is...I want $100,000.00 in small bills to be deposited in the Barclay Bank. In 15 calendar days I will hold a press conference to announce that your company won the contract."

It was cloudy that June morning when Donald Fitzroy filed a petition to compel the Court to reveal the name of the state's star confidential witness. Judge Lassiter denied the petition *prima facie*, thus narrowing the margin of error for the defense.

Contrary to the Councilman's public stance, Vincent Cochran could no longer remain optimistic about the outcome. Vincent didn't know who or why someone would want to set him up and no longer cared. The damage was already done. It wasn't long before Vincent began to withdraw from public view-sinking into a merciless depression. Ashamed of what he had become after being bestowed with his district's trust. His efforts had been suddenly sidelined by an unknown force that seemed determined to destroy his effectiveness.

He began moping around the house in his bathrobe. Getting dressed had become a chore. Family and friends worried that Vincent might do something harmful to himself, so the decision was made that someone should accompany the disgraced councilman everywhere he went. This unwanted attention led to episodes of hide-and-seek between Vincent and those closest to him. The most recent being after Vinnie was informed by Donald Fitzroy that Judge Lassiter had ruled in favor of the State. This meant that the councilman's bribery trial would begin before he left office. Angered by the decision, Vinnie took off running and disappeared into a dense Manhattan crowd. A cousin, who had accompanied Vincent to Fitzroy's office, searched for more than an hour before he found Vinnie sipping coffee in a Nathan's restaurant nearby.

Reggie decided that with all the confusion going on with his brother, he should slow down his relationship with cover model Sylvia Mitchell. They had met each other a few months prior, while attending a charity fund raiser at the Whitney Museum. She was on the arm of millionaire art dealer, Warren Rice, who was 90 years old and in frail health.

Sylvia cried as Reggie broke the news to her, but perked up once he disclosed his desire to marry her when things died down. Vincent summoned Fitzroy along with Fitzroy's personal case investigator, Rory Howard, his brother, Reggie and Chief of Staff Charles Fuller for drinks at his home. After small talk about current events, Vincent steered the conversation towards his personal problems.

Holding up a letter for identification, Vinnie said, "I got a telegram from the Governor of the Grand Cayman Islands. A jury found Roy Wendell guilty of murdering Judy Bernstein. They scheduled his hanging for next week."

Everyone in the room was silently relieved at the news. This was a small win for Vinnie Cochran. The public could begin putting its trust in him again. Donald looked in the direction of his investigator, Rory Howard, giving him the sign that it was time to explain their progress.

Rory described his painstaking hunt to locate the whereabouts of the state's star witness as "fruitless," and suggested that the D.A.'s was stashing the witness away with an clear demand that said: Do not open until the trial date. Reliable sources were uncharacteristically tight-lipped about the location of the safe house and the exact time the witness would be transferred to the courthouse. The D.A. issued a directive that anyone proven to have leaked or supplied information relating to the location and transportation of the witness in the People v. Cochran trial would be prosecuted to the full extent of the law.

"We should have stolen the evidence from the D.A.'s office," Reggie suggested.

"Are you kidding?" Vincent said, "Those records are bolted to the fucking D.A.'s desk. Nobody's getting their hands on them."

"What if the State's claims are just that—claims, allegations and non-factual," asked Charles Fuller.

"Oh, to the contrary, they do have substance," Fitzroy interjected. "Bank records, serial numbers and the personal markings of the witness on the $100,000.00 which verifies a transaction to the Barclay bank. Believe me," Fitzroy added, "I have copies of these documents, so there is a case."

"How does it look for my brother, Don?" Reggie asked.

"I'm sorry to tell you, Reggie," Fitzroy said, "but it doesn't look good for Vincent. You know how to pray, right?"

Scratching his head, Vinnie said, "I do know this: when that money appeared in my account, whoever did this facilitated the appearance of a bribe."

Not only did it appear that a bribe was accepted, the Internal Revenue Service believed that no share of the $100,000.00 was set aside for them—which triggered an investigation to find out if tax evasion had occurred.

The bribery trial for the People v. Cochran began February 28th, 1979. Ten days prior to the jury being paneled, the D.A. made his first offer to Vincent: 1 to 3 years plus a lifetime ban from public service.

"No way," Vincent declared. He couldn't imagine living life without politics. Vincent had to fight. He would let the marbles fall where they may.

The State began its case by calling the secret star witness. A hush blanketed the courtroom as the witness, protected by a human curtain of court officers, was ushered to the witness box. It wasn't until he took the stand that Vincent, for the first time, was able to see his accuser. When he sat and lifted his head, he revealed himself to be none other than David Markoff.

Dressed immaculately in a white three-piece suit, three quarter high white kangaroo shoes and a white panama hat-held in his hand, Markoff resembled the Chinese celluloid detective Charlie Chan.

There were greetings in the direction of family and friends he hadn't seen in months and to members of the press who sought interviews from the reclusive deponent. Markoff remained pleasant and jovial, as he explained to the jury how he became involved in the Hugo View project. He described how Councilman Cochran boasted that his clout with co-members of the council committee on Land Use would cost him $100,000.0—an inference that Vincent could use his clout and the money to steer the project to him.

After four days on the witness stand, David Markoff had established himself as a credible witness, scoring points with the jury almost instantly. Before the second witness could be called, which would be a Barclay Bank official, Vincent had heard enough and firmly instructed his lawyer that he would accept the previously offered 1-3 year plea with a lifetime ban from politics. Eager to remove People v. Cochran from the court calendar, ADA Carluchi and Judge Lassiter concurred.

The State had accomplished both its objectives: The trial had a speedy resolution and the fact that Markoff had bribed Housing and Preservation Development inspectors in the past to cover up violations never came out-saving the ADA considerable embarrassment.

It had only been a month since Vincent had to seriously consider retirement—when Donald Fitzroy posed that question to him. Fitzroy's astute advice was delivered poetically as he told his client, "Cowards forge ahead to disguise their lack of true grit. However, real men know when retreat is at the fore."

Had Vincent been a younger man he would have fought fiercely to save his name and career. Sadly, older and already wounded as a result of mounting stress and humiliation, he was in no shape for the dog-eat-dog bribery trial. His fortitude was depleted and his vitality was nearly gone.

Not only had Vincent begun displaying distance towards his ordinarily close staff, he blew up at his secretary for transferring a WCBS radio reporter's call to him after he had specifically instructed her to "hold all calls." The last straw was when Vincent accused Charles Fuller, his faithful Chief of Staff, of being part of the conspiracy to remove him from the City Council.

Joel Bernstein had exposed Vincent to the good in public service, but Vincent wasn't prepared for the murky events looming ahead and it was beginning to show. The dirty tricks and posturing of New York City politics required a mental toughness that Vincent no longer could even pretend to possess.

Subsequently, Vincent signed the papers confirming his acceptance of the plea bargain agreement. Meanwhile, Reggie departed for Bali in what he called an attempt to "get my mind right and get back on the right road."

Upon Reggie's return, he received a bill from Donald Fitzroy and his partners. The $201,000.000 bill was sent to Reggie instead of Vincent because the IRS had made its intentions known that it would launch a full-scale audit of Vincent's finances. And, with those intentions, the agency froze his accounts at Barclay and Chemical banks.

Still, Vincent maintained his freedom when his lawyers delayed his formal sentencing as they explored appeal possibilities. Many legal pundits agreed that Vincent could argue ineffective counsel on the premise that Donald was indeed a contract attorney who practiced criminal law on an average of two or three times per year. These facts would render Attorney Fitzroy ineffective to his client-who sought to have his basic fundamental rights protected. Others countered with the fact that Councilman Cochran, after lengthy consultation on his rights and options, agreed to a sentence of 3 years in prison in return for his plea to acceptance of a bribe-a felony in the State of New York.

When Judge Lassiter learned about the ploy, he ordered the disgraced councilman and his inept barrister to appear in his courtroom at 10:00 a.m. on Tuesday April 2nd. And when the obstinate duo arrived, Judge Lassiter tore into them for using "tactics aimed at circumventing due process" in an effort to evade a mutually agreed upon plea bargain.

"You should be ashamed of yourself," the judge scolded Fitzroy. "You're a disgrace to your district and to the city at large. With the eyes of the world focused on this case and this system of jurisprudence, you've allowed this city a window into the corrupt machinery of local government.

"As of this moment, you, Vincent Cochran, are to be transferred to the custody of the N.Y.S. Department of Corrections to be dealt with as they see fit. I, Judge Lassiter, sentence you to an indeterminate term not to exceed 3 years, with a minimum of 1 year-to be coupled with a lifetime ban from public office."

Reggie felt terrible about Judge Lassiter's decision to remand Vincent. He blamed the whole thing on Donald Fitzroy. It was Fitzroy's responsibility to construct a legal strategy that wouldn't offend the court, and to a lesser degree, the judge.

First, Lassiter was willing to postpone the trial until the councilman's term was over. If ADA Carluchi hadn't opposed the decision with an order to show cause, the decision might have stood. Not a mean-spirited man, Judge Lassiter allowed the councilman a few weeks to get his business in order before reporting to prison.

With his brother behind bars, Reggie felt lost—especially because his financial stability was completely blown to bits. His on-again-off-again relationship with Sylvia Mitchell was on again to the degree that she allowed him to move into her United Nations Plaza apartment. The couple cruised all the clubs frequented by celebrity types, stealing the attention reserved for social blue bloods, record producers and avant garde musicians, painters and sculptors. Pictured on several occasions in the society section of the New York Daily News and the New York Post, Reggie and Sylvia quickly became a well-known item.

Ironically, these same clubs were the haunts frequented by David Markoff who had walked into the Bronx District attorney's office in 1977 and set a series of events into motion that would eventually lead to the conviction and downfall of a New York City councilman and provide total immunity for himself.

For the next four years Reggie struggled to maintain a steady income. He was unable to rely on Vincent, a convicted felon-banned from New York City politics, who became the proprietor of a bed & breakfast in Island Pond, Vermont after his release.

At a loss for what to do to solve his money problems, Reggie contemplated returning to North Carolina, but changed his mind because of Sylvia. She was the ideal mate and put no pressure on him. Sylvia enjoyed Reggie's company and sexual fulfillment so much that they were married in September 1983.

On a cold December morning as Sylvia packed her suitcase for a modeling assignment in Madagascar—where Reggie would accompany her—he abruptly changed his mind. He told her he had an urgent meeting with Donald Fitzroy about legal bills. An argument ensued and Sylvia left for Africa all alone.

When she returned Reggie wasn't home. There was no sign of him or any written messages left for her to find.

'I'm not gonna panic,' she told herself. But after Reggie failed to return all weekend, Sylvia reported him missing to the police. Just as she was giving police a description of her now-missing husband, Reggie walked through the door.

"Where the hell you been?" Sylvia yelled. "I've been worried sick about you," Sylvia declared, dropping the phone as she ran into Reggie's arms, relieved that her man was home safe and sound.

"I had a couple of errands to take care of," Reggie said matter-of-factly.

"I've been here since Friday evening," Sylvia explained, with her right hand on her curvy hip. "Here it is, Sunday and you couldn't call to let me know you were alright?"

Reggie stood silently, wearing a blank look on his face as his loving wife continued. "I'm on the phone describing to the cops what you look like, and then you walk in like all you did was pick up the newspaper."

"I'm sorry if I worried you," Reggie said opening the refrigerator and pouring a glass of orange juice. "I should've called. I'm sorry sweetheart."

"Did you talk to Donald?"

"Huh? Oh yeah."

"Well...what happened?"

"He apologized for any undue mental stress and explained that it was a simple mistake made when one of the secretaries in the firm billed me by accident instead of Vinnie."

"You believe that?" Sylvia asked skeptically.

"Fuck no! Reggie said. "They know my brother filed for bankruptcy in Vermont. They were probing to see if I was willing to pay the bill."

The following evening, while Reggie and Sylvia relaxed at home, reports came over the evening news revealing that a fire had extensively damaged the law firm of Fitzroy, Ludlow & Scott.

Sylvia became concerned when the news that the firm of the attorney that had represented her brother-in-law against bribery charges was totally destroyed by fire didn't garner any reaction from Reggie. An uncomfortable feeling began to settle in her thoughts and in her stomach. Had Reggie been involved in something so sinister during that weekend while she was in Madagascar that her relationship with him could be totally jeopardized?

Sylvia's suspicions were confirmed a week later as she was backstage preparing to model Homiko Torres' spring fashion line. She was informed that her husband had been arrested for arson in connection with the law firm fire.

The judge shocked everyone present in the courtroom that day when she set bail at $1 million, casting serious doubt on Reggie's intent on recapturing his freedom. Reggie's reluctance to pin down his whereabouts during the weekend of the law firm fire gradually influenced Sylvia's notion about her husband's involvement in the crime. The leather tote bag she had given Reggie as a gift was missing. Could that bag have contained clues to what Reggie was up to that weekend?

Sylvia worried about how Reggie would have reacted if he ever became aware of the reason she couldn't generate enough funds to bail him out and pay for his defense. It was because she had already paid Donald Fitzroy's law firm the $201,000.00 it was owed and she was, as a result, nearly broke.

During his trial, which began June 1st, 1984, Reggie was frequently surprised by the appearance of his long-time friend, Terry Williams and his beautiful wife, Vivian, who made the trip from their home in Vernon, New Jersey. News of Reggie's arrest was practically nonexistent in the newspapers Terry and Vivian read. They found out through a letter they received from Vincent Cochran. Vinnie was still living in Vermont and wanted to support his brother personally, but experienced a barrage of media attention during his appearance at jury selection. Terry and Viv's non-celebrity status would prove invaluable to all interested parties. They served as personal correspondents to Vincent back in Vermont and as provider of moral support for Reggie and Sylvia in the courtroom.

On July 17th, seven weeks after the trial had begun; Reggie was convicted of conspiracy of arson. Once those Reggie hired were caught, confessed to the crime and to Reggie's involvement as conspirator, he was sentenced to 8 to 25 years in prison.

The documentary's narrator somberly concluded: "At no other moment in U.S. political history or in the annals of crime, has it been chronicled that two brothers—one elected to the city council, the other a member of his staff—have been convicted of a crime, respectively. Those dual crimes harvested the term, *Bribe & Burn,* which symbolized the brother's contribution of malfeasance and subsequent reprisal during their brief stint in City Hall."

CHAPTER SEVEN

Meet Baron Von Mickva

One month after the "Bribe & Burn" documentary aired, Reggie and Terry were flown to a Las Vegas Country Club in a private plane piloted by Jaco Philips.

After they landed, a limo taxied them to a 90 foot yacht anchored in picturesque Lake Mead. The owner of the private plane and yacht was none other than Baron Von Mickva. The Baron, dressed in a floral short-sleeved shirt and white linen shorts, resembled the consummate host.

"Welcome gentleman. Welcome," The Baron said. "I've been waiting for you. Climb aboard."

Aboard the yacht, The Baron led the trio down a small set of stairs located a stone's throw away from the Captain's stateroom. The Salvatore Ferragamo sofa and Elton John autographed piano parked inside the lower deck provided a whisper of pop sophistication.

"So, I finally get to meet the infamous Reggie Cochran, huh?" Von Mickva said. "I saw the documentary about you and your brother. Some story. Very informative."

"Thanks, but I'm impressed to finally meet you, Baron. You the man," Reggie answered respectfully.

Von Mickva summoned one of his servants to fetch the drinks requested by his guests: Reggie, a Jim Bean on the rocks; Terry and Jaco, Smirnoff with cranberry juice; while The Baron, a non-alcoholic sipper, had a glass of apricot nectar.

One of Von Mickva's assistants handed out folders to Terry and Reggie outlining the backgrounds of Jaco and The Baron.

Reggie and Terry were indeed impressed. The Baron, with Jaco as his lieutenant, had financed and participated in militant and revolutionary coups during the 1960's. These insurgencies were designed to increase civil unrest in four Islamic countries, namely Lebanon, Syria, Iran, and Yemen.

While The Baron highlighted Jaco Philips' raw talent for extracting information, Jaco basked in the praise being bestowed upon him. Between the Middle East and his involvement with the Black Panthers in his Philadelphia hometown, Jaco's dossier was a hefty three hundred and fifty pages.

"Jaco, you're too damn qualified for this operation. What the fuck haven't you done?" Reggie inquired, showcasing that ever present wicked smile.

After pondering for a few seconds, Jaco answered, "You know, there's not much I haven't done, but I have to tell ya' this...I would love to do this project. The stuff I did with the Panthers and most recently, with The Baron were for different reasons, man. However, your project-if The Baron wasn't paying me-I'd do for free."

"When Reggie and I spoke on the phone last week," The Baron interjected, "I took the liberty of expressing your determined interests in working with Jaco."

"You mean you guys already talked about this stuff?" Terry asked.

"Oh, yes. We're eager to get started," The Baron insisted, taking a sip of his apricot nectar.

"Okay, this is the deal. There are three parole commissioners in New York State that act as a team of venom-filled serpents, who—for years before my incarceration—have sought to re-punish inmates convicted of infamous crimes. They refused me parole, mandating me to stay until my conditional release date," Reggie explained. "As for my brother, Vincent, they just fucked with his mind, threatening to void his release until they finally relented. He wrote me letters during that period describing his personal anguish. It ate me up inside, man. You just don't know," Reggie shook his head to hold back the tears that threatened to leak from his eyes.

"I hate those three fucks to no end," he continued. "They've had a long run out there. I want them to suffer to the magnitude of those they've condemned."

"Terry, since I sent you the money, has there been any problems?" The Baron asked.

"No. The holding facility should be complete by the end of the week," Terry said. "I don't anticipate any problems with the equipment we ordered for Jaco last month," Terry said. "So the only thing left to do is pick up our guests before the party starts."

"What do you know about their routines?" Jaco asked.

"We know that the parole commissioners drive their own cars to the state office in Albany Monday through Thursday," Terry said. "A state vehicle shuttles them to the facilities for hearings, then returns them to the state headquarters where they drive themselves home at the end of the day. It's between those stops that we have to snatch them assholes," Terry added.

"Do you think it's possible to have the details rounded out in the next two months?" Von Mickva inquired.

"What do you think, Terry?" Reggie asked.

"I think so," said Terry, lifting his body to change his sitting position.

"Excellent," The Baron said. "I'll be in New York when my fighter, Simon Davis, puts his heavyweight championship on the line at Madison Square Garden's Felt Forum in two months. We can go over all the details at that time. I'm inviting you both to be my special guests for the evening. Bring your wives if you want," Von Mickva added.

"Really?" Terry asked.

"Absolutely! That's what these events are all about. Come on out and have a good time, and in the process get some business accomplished," The Baron replied.

"Sounds good, Mr. Von Mickva," Reggie said. "I will work out the details and get in touch with you in a few weeks."

"Good. I'm glad," The Baron said rising from his chair. "Now, I can hit the links and shoot a few holes. Coming, Jaco?"

"Yes. I think will," Jaco said. "You guys are welcome."

"Thanks, but no thanks," Terry said, standing to his feet. "Reggie and I have a flight out this evening. Maybe next time, huh?"

"I'm gonna hold you to that offer," Jaco said.

Reggie and Terry left Las Vegas feeling quite comfortable about their impending joint venture with The Baron and Jaco.

CHAPTER EIGHT

One Helluva Week

The rain came down in buckets the following week, flooding the streets below Reggie's apartment. Cochran was sleeping peacefully until two automobiles skidded through a traffic light across the street from his bedroom window. The phone rang. He reached to the night table to pick it up.

"We got a problem," Jaco said in a desperate tone.

"What's that?" A puzzled Reggie inquired.

"The workers have finished your chateau, but there's one snag," Jaco said. "Are you ready? Pavulon."

"Would you repeat that again?"

"Pavulon. We can't use the gurney without it."

"Ooohhh, that's the muscle relaxer Terry told me about," Reggie said. "I thought Terry received the equipment we needed already?"

"He thought so, too. But one of the workers at the site checking the deliveries noticed that the Pavulon hadn't arrived. Apparently someone fucked up on the delivery," Jaco replied. "He called me two days ago explaining the problem. I told him I could fix it, so I flew in yesterday."

Jaco continued to explain to Reggie that he knew where he could get his hands on the drug.

Located in a rural town seventy miles east of Minneapolis' Northern Lake Hospital was the largest single supply of Pavulon in the U.S.

Jaco expounded that he was close friends with Dr. Evelyn Yogami, Chief of Pharmaceuticals at Northern Lake. He told Reggie that he could divert her attention upon a visit to the hospital.

Reggie and Jaco boarded a United Airlines flight from Newark Airport bound for Minneapolis the next morning. Terry wasn't able to make the trip. Vivian no longer approved of her husband's close relationship with Reggie and began nagging him to break their ties—starting with the Minnesota trip.

Vivian had noticed Reggie running around the city, calling people, and meeting with people, traveling and making all kinds of secretive deals. She was concerned that he was planning something she didn't want her Terry involved in. This matter, in turn, became the subject of frequent arguments between Vivian and Terry.

When flight 711 landed in Minneapolis, Reggie and Jaco took a cab to the closest flea bag motel they could find, one appropriately called The Dump. Fresh off the heels of the televised documentary, "Bribe & Burn", Reggie was plotting his movements, making every effort to not be recognized.

Jaco called his friend, Dr. Yogami, at the hospital. She was enthusiastic and surprised to hear from Jaco, saying that she couldn't wait to see him. The hospital was very hectic at that time, so Dr. Yogami informed Jaco to come around during the evening shift when activity slows down.

Reggie and Jaco had to wait, but Reggie was becoming impatient. He wanted to know more about what Jaco was going to do once they got to the hospital.

"You don't trust me, do you?" Jaco asked.

Staring Jaco in the eyes, Reggie said, "I just met you a few months ago. Trusting you hasn't come into play yet, Jaco. Right now we're working. I know this operation is my responsibility, my baby. I appreciate you and the Baron's contribution. However, this is real and I won't get stuck with both thumbs in my ass at no hospital."

"Ha-ha-ha. You're a funny motherfucker, ain't you, Reggie?" Jaco asked. "Okay, let's go over the plan."

"Yeah, let's do that."

Jaco pulled up a chair while Reggie relaxed on the bed and began to explain.

"Dr. Yogami and I met in 1990 at the University of Pennsylvania. She was speaking at a conference on pharmaceutical security. Actually, I was there for a gun show in Harrisburg and noticed a flyer on the ground. I picked it up, read it, saw her pretty face touting the event, got in my car and drove to the university. At the conference we locked eyes and later met at a nearby campus pub. She drank quite freely, so I generously brought her vodka and tonics," Jaco said with a chuckle.

"Naturally, Dr. Yogami got drunk on her ass and invited me to her apartment. We had sex, great sex. So great, I thought about settling down with her in St. Paul."

Jaco's intimate admission left Reggie amused and speechless. But after a few moments, Reggie said, "You like to live and work where the action is. You wouldn't last two weeks in that place. There's nothing for you in Minnesota."

"You don't understand," Jaco said. "Evelyn is Egyptian. She graduated from the University of Cairo-sixth on the list. She's a hard worker who doesn't engage in sex very often—you know, the serious type. Then, she meets me and on the first night she chooses to become intimate with me. I had to consider changing my plans," Jaco laughed. "I ain't gonna lie. Shit."

"How long did it last?" Reggie asked.

"A year," said Jaco, looking down at his clasped hands.

"A year? Only one year and you were ready to change your life for this woman?" Reggie said, laughing out loud. "I don't know you well, but I can tell that you fall in love quickly."

"So what. It's my only human flaw," Jaco said. "I'm certainly not alone."

"No, no you're not," Reggie said. "But can we get back to the plan? I want to see how you can use your past affection and turn it into a clever ruse to get Pavulon."

"Simple. I thought about it on the way here. Look, she told me that whenever I'm in the Minnesota area to drop by. Well, I'm about to drop in on her in a big way," he said, smiling.

"There are two supply rooms for pharmaceuticals at Northern Lake Hospital. The largest one is on the first floor. The second, a smaller supply, room is connected to Dr. Yogami's office on the sixth floor," Jaco explained. "While I'm inside with Dr. Yogami getting reacquainted, give me twenty minutes then crawl on your hands and knees, past us and unlock the door and take the Pavulon," he told Reggie, who was listening intently.

"Don't pay attention to what the good doctor and I are engaged in, it will only slow you down," Jaco said. He handed Reggie two code/search/rip swipe cards to enter the pharmaceutical supply room."

"This had better work, Mr. Philips," Reggie added.

"Northern Lake Hospital has been cited for several violations," Jaco said. "Two years ago they lost their accreditation and still, it's very lax there. Don't worry. We'll be outta there in thirty minutes tops," he said, patting Reggie on the back.

"I sure hope so," Reggie said apprehensively.

As dusk settled upon the dry Minnesota skies, Reggie and Jaco arrived at Northern Lake Hospital about the time Dr. Yogami advised, when it was practically empty.

Upon exiting the elevator on the sixth floor, they walked down the hollow, unoccupied corridor stopping briefly near a supply closet.

"Put this on," Jaco said, handing Reggie a white lab coat, "just in case somebody comes by."

"Well, I'm going in," Jaco said with a smile on his face. "Remember, give me twenty minutes then enter."

Reggie nodded his head in compliance. Suddenly alone on the sixth floor, Reggie proceeded towards the men's room. But before entering, he affixed an Out of Order sign to the bathroom door to distract others from utilizing it.

Reggie assumed it was safer waiting in the bathroom for his synchronized cue rather than in the corridor. He felt very awkward in a lab coat pacing up and down the halls. His ignorance to the medical profession left him feeling ineffective in terms of portraying hospital staff. Besides, Reggie felt like a character from one of Tom Clancy's novels-donning a lab coat and lying in wait for his cue.

A look at his watch indicated that eighteen minutes had elapsed. Almost time to begin. Reggie set his mind on getting ready for action.

As soon as Reggie placed his hand on the door knob to Dr. Yogami's office, he felt the weight of a heavy hand on his shoulder.

"Do you work on this floor?" a nurse asked.

"Oh no, uh uh. I'm on the fourth floor, but I have to get some medication from Dr. Yogami's office," Reggie stammered.

"I know you're in a rush, but would you be a sweetheart and help us put this gurney on the elevator? We're just going down to the fifth floor. You can ride right back up. Please?" the nurse begged.

"I don't know," Reggie said apprehensively, "I am in a hurry."

"Oh, please," the nurse repeated as if she wouldn't take no for an answer. Reggie was reluctant to help the pushy nurse, but he didn't want to alert those accompanying her that he might not work in this hospital at all. He figured that with two minutes to spare he would be able to help them and then shoot back up to Dr. Yogami's office in time to unlock the door, get the Pavulon, then leave unannounced.

On the elevator he went, pushing the gurney with one hand and checking the time with the other.

When the elevator opened, in one combined motion Reggie firmly pushed the gurney out and fingered the button to the sixth floor.

The nurse only got to say, "Aren't you gonna..." before the doors met and the elevator rocketed to the sixth floor.

He ran down the hall, swiped the door to Dr. Yogami's office and entered the room. He tipped-toed passed the semi-naked bodies of Jaco and the good doctor cavorting on the couch near the supply room. He then swiped the electronic lock next to the supply room and looked inside, "Pavulon...it's everywhere," he whispered under his breath.

The duo met up later at the hotel, grabbed their clothes, checked out and caught a red eye flight back to New York City.

The following Thursday, heavyweight champion Simon Davis and challenger Lindsay McKoy weighed in at the Felt Forum's media room for their title bout on Saturday. Baron Von Mickva kept the event interesting, hyping his fighter, Simon Davis as the "Hercules" of the boxing world.

"Lindsay McKoy doesn't have a chance in hell", Von Mickva said. "He knows he doesn't have a chance and all of you do, too," he added, pointing in the reporters' direction. "His ass is showing up merely to collect his paycheck!"

It was widely known in the boxing community that Baron Von Mickva had a reputation for neglecting his fighters and no fighter was neglected more than his top moneymaker, Simon Davis. Even though The Baron had promoted fights for hundreds of boxers, it was Davis who made the Baron a household name.

So as the Baron's limousine drove Simon to his luxury suite at the Plaza Hotel after the weigh in, Simon felt compelled to inform the Baron of something he was doing.

"I hired an accountant," Simon announced.

"You did what?" The Baron asked, raising his voice.

"I-I hired an accountant."

"For what?"

"That's a good question," Simon said. I don't know what triggered it exactly, but I do know one thing..."

"And that is?"

"You been robbing me for some time now. Oh yeah. And I want all my money back."

"Or what?" The Baron interrupted. What'cha gonna do, Simon, take it from me, huh?"

A surprised-looking Davis just stared at The Baron.

"Go in my pocket and take it," The Baron dared. "You know I keep large sums of money on me. Remember your old sparring partner, Zale Stewart?" The Baron asked, changing the subject.

"God bless, Stew. I miss him," Simon lamented.

"Yeah, I know. Me too. It was such a loss. I told everybody that it must have been a coincidence that Stew died just after an argumentative meeting with me," The Baron stated angrily. "And I wouldn't want anything to happen to you, too. You know...not with the fight and all."

Looking at the sick smile on The Baron's face, Simon knew that he was hearing an indirect confession about Zale Stewart's demise and that his future could mirror Stew's.

"Don't ever threaten me again. You hear me, Simon?" The Baron snarled. "You wouldn't possess a heavyweight title if it wasn't for me," The Baron said, pointing at himself. "I'm a deal maker. If it wasn't for me you'd still be pumping gas in Oklahoma."

This was the sort of relationship the Baron had with several of his fighters. "Don't question me. Just be thrilled that you're part of the family," Von Mickva would often tell them. And the fighters were well aware of the retaliation The Baron was capable of unleashing. Although the depth of his involvement with terrorists was unknown, his participation wasn't exactly a secret.

It was just that mutual infamy that brought Reggie and Von Mickva together. But in sharp contrast, Reggie's main honcho, Terry, and his wife Vivian seemed to be falling apart. Vivian's assumptions about Reggie's mission, coupled with her fears about Terry's role in that mission and the seedy cast of characters they had begun hanging out with was putting a major strain on their marriage.

"So, have you told him?" Vivian asked Terry as they sat together in their living room. "No. Not yet," Terry replied somberly.

"Well, when are you planning to tell him, huh?" Vivian snapped.

"When the time is right," Terry answered. "Who knows? Maybe I won't tell at all," he added defiantly.

"What?" Vivian yelled. "You said that you would! Never mind. Just forget about it," Vivian said crossing her arms across her chest.

"I know what I said, but guess what? Maybe I changed my mind and I don't wanna do it now," Terry said sarcastically.

"You know what I think. I think you're scared of Reggie."

"Ha! Scared? I'm not scared of Reggie. He's my best friend-we grew up together," Terry said.

"That's was a long, long time ago baby. He's changed," Vivian said, relaxing her arms and placing her hands on her lap.

"What the fuck are you talking about? How has he changed, Vivian?" Terry responded.

"Listen, Honey," Vivian said. "Reggie was much more focused on the right things when he was younger. But now he's hell bent on administering revenge on those parole commissioners and I don't want you getting involved in his obsessions."

"Obsessions?" Terry said, chuckling into his glass of wine. "That's what you think this is all about? No wonder you've been acting like this. He's my friend. Reggie is a good man. He just took a couple of wrong turns in his life, that's all."

"Like hell he took a couple of wrong turns," Vivian said. "Reggie doesn't have a damn steering wheel, Baby."

"Oh, come on, Viv. That's my friend you're talking about. I wish you would put your opinion aside-at least for this evening. We're going to the fight, you know."

"You're lucky I'm a boxing fan or we'd be talking about this a little longer."

Terry chose to diffuse the conversation by not replying as he walked passed Vivian to the bedroom.

When the chauffeur rang the doorbell at 7:15 p.m., Terry and Vivian had resolved their differences enough to accompany a stylishly dressed Reggie Cochran to Madison Square Garden's Felt Forum for Simon Davis' championship bout as V.I.P. guests of Baron Von Mickva.

Von Mickva was busy visiting with Davis in his dressing room and giving him the routine pep talk.

"Are you ready? I hope you are?" The Baron declared, rubbing his hands together nervously. "This is when we earn our money."

"Of course," Simon said half-smiling, while getting his hands taped by his trainer. "Have all the loose ends been tied up?"

"Oh, yes, I visited privately with the judges in their hotel rooms to guard against any confusion," The Baron said. "I instructed them to look for every opportunity to amass points in your favor," Von Mickva said confidently.

"Whew! I'm glad Baron," Simon said. "I don't wanna let you down.

"I know, Simon," Von Mickva said. "Believe me...he knows you can't really fight a lick. I'm paying Lindsay McKoy enough to not seriously hurt you or take your title."

A good night's sleep was all Simon Davis needed to realize that he was nothing without The Baron's guidance. With that realization, Davis terminated his accountant's services and promptly apologized to Von Mickva before the fight for any harm he caused.

The Felt Forum had been converted from a 7,000 seat venue to a 10,000 seat boxing arena complete with bronze railings and gothic decor. A $2 million filtration system kept clean air circulating throughout events. Sky boxes, located above ringside, allowed the powerfully rich and famous to observe the action from an ultra-secure area.

"You don't know how thrilled I am that you three are here to witness history in the making," Von Mickva said to Reggie, Terry and Vivian in the comfort of the sky box he co-owns with Abner Hill, CEO of Amalgamated Oil. "Never in the annals of boxing history has a promoter, like me, made so much money with so little talent. It just boggles my mind," he said, laughing.

"Really?" Reggie asked.

"Yes indeed. You know it reminds me of a story my father told me about a little girl who wanted to sell her pretty doll," Von Mickva told his guests. "But no one would buy it because one of the doll's arms was missing. So, the next day she brought the doll out in a box that concealed the missing arm. Finally, someone bought it."

"What's your point?" Reggie asked.

"Yeah. I want to know, too," Vivian said.

"You can sell anything. It's all in the packaging, the presentation. Pronounce the positives. Withhold the negatives. Then sell, sell, sell," The Baron said.

"Interesting concept, but what are you trying to say, Baron? Simon Davis can't fight or what?" Reggie asked.

"You think I would have people witness a fight that my guy loses? Give me more credit than that," The Baron chuckled.

"Hey, I'm just asking, you know," Reggie said.

"I beg your pardon. I produce high quality boxing matches," The Baron added.

"That's why we're here. None of us doubt you. Shit, we never even heard of Lindsay McKoy," Reggie added.

"Isn't Simon undefeated, Baron?" Vivian inquired.

"Absolutely," The Baron answered confidently. "I see why you married this beautiful lady, Terry, she's very knowledgeable."

Once the bell rang signaling the start of the fight, the audience was treated to a gladiator's match. Lindsay wasted no time being the aggressor, keeping Davis peddling backwards to avoid real contact.

Between rounds, Reggie rushed to a concession stand for a drink. While on the line he recognized a familiar voice.

"So, this is where I have to be if I wanna catch up with you, huh?" Sylvia said. She was happily surprised to bump into Reggie after a long hiatus of the past several months.

"Sylvia," Reggie replied smiling. "What a surprise to see you here."

"Enough with the bullshit, Reggie," she snapped. "Why have you been duckin' me, huh?"

"I haven't been duckin' you," Reggie fired back, "Who are you here with?"

"Don't change the subject," Sylvia replied. "We fucked each other and you disappeared," Sylvia charged.

"I didn't like the idea of you sleeping with me while your entire family was at home, that's all," Reggie said.

"You could have called and expressed your disapproval," Sylvia said. "I've been leaving messages and faxes at that big house you own upstate. And I even reached out to Terry, too. Didn't I tell you?" Sylvia asked.

"Who told you about me owning a house upstate?" Reggie asked, his eyes bulging.

"Oh, that," Sylvia replied nonchalantly.

"Yeah, that," Reggie snapped back, pulling Sylvia off the concession stand line and towards a more obscure area.

"Ooww, let me go, Reggie! You're hurting me."

"Not until you tell me what I wanna know," Reggie growled.

The anger reflected in Reggie's eyes made Sylvia aware that he was quite serious about his request.

"No one told me anything," Sylvia said.

"Stop lying," Reggie insisted. "Then how did you find out?" Reggie asked, looking around to observe who was paying attention to their pressure-packed conversation.

"Like I told you earlier, I wanted to see you. I missed you. I got tired of sitting by the phone," she admitted. "And since Terry wouldn't give me any information, I followed Terry one night after he left a restaurant. I had no idea where he was headed until he drove into the driveway of this lovely upstate mansion. I still had no idea who owned the place," she said.

Reggie remained silent throughout Sylvia's testimony. He wasn't about to interrupt her. He wanted to know what else Sylvia knew about his plan.

"I asked the landscaper," Sylvia continued. "And he described you to a tee. I had to practically pull his teeth just to get that little bit of information," she said. "He wouldn't tell anything else. He was loyal."

"How loyal could he be if he told you who owns that house?" Reggie shook his index finger centimeters away from Sylvia's beautiful kisser and said, "Bitch, stay out of my fucking way!" He pushed Sylvia and stormed away.

When the seventh round ended, two out of three judges had Davis ahead. In the interim, between the 7th and 8th rounds, Simon's trainer reassured him that all was under control and that all he had to do was to keep his guard up and stick the jab. The Baron would take care of the rest. That reassurance gave Davis a reason to smile.

Reggie paced the arena's corridor fuming. His mind swirled with questions about Sylvia Mitchell's nosey ways. He suddenly noticed the presence of Jaco Phillips in the building about 25 feet away talking in a determined tone on the telephone. Jaco barked instructions into the receiver, pen in one hand and a piece of paper in the other.

"Did I miss anything?" Reggie asked Terry when he arrived back in his seat.

"Of course. It's boxing," Vivian answered.

"I'm not gonna respond to that," Reggie said.

"We thought you got lost," The Baron said.

"No, unfortunately I ran into somebody I knew," Reggie said with a stiff grin on his face.

During the twelfth and final round, angry words were exchanged between fans of Lindsay McKoy, who was seated directly behind Simon Davis' corner, and Davis' cut man, Eddie. One fan in particular didn't like the fact that Terry's wife had been permitted to stand with the Davis camp. Words ensued and another jealous fan threw a large cup of soda, which landed squarely on Vivian's beige silk dress.

Unaware of the quagmire that was unfolding in his corner, Davis threw a barrage of left and right hooks and other combinations to the head and body of Lindsay, leaving McKoy out on his feet. When Davis got his chance to look in the direction of his corner, he witnessed his 68 year old cut man being slammed with a chair repeatedly over the head. Vivian, with television cameras focused on her, sprayed mace at fans while she cursed them to the level of a sailor on leave.

Soon other fans joined the melee and punches were coming from everywhere. The area around Davis' corner was a madhouse with people throwing punches. One of those punches was landed on Vivian's jaw and dropped her flat.

Pushing, shoving and, in some cases, stepping over spectators who stood in his way, Terry sliced through the dense crowd to come to Vivian's aid. She lay barely moving on the floor below Simon Davis' corner.

"Baby? Baby? Are you alright?" Terry asked cradling his wife in his arms. He let out a sigh of relief when Vivian began to open her eyes.

"Somebody sucker-punched me, Honey. I feel light-headed, Vivian answered.

"Terry, I'm sorry about all this," said Simon, leaning over the ring ropes, "I wanted you to witness real boxing-not this."

"Hey, it's not your fault. You're not security. Besides, you were great in there. You probably won," Terry said.

Davis simply nodded his head to concur.

After Terry consulted with on-site doctors, it was decided that Vivian should be taken to a local hospital to be checked out along with Davis' cut man, Eddie, who sustained a serious head injury.

Not until security regained order and the injured were carted off to local hospitals could the winner of the fight be announced: Davis Defeats McKoy by Unanimous Decision.

"The doctor said you suffered a mild concussion. You can go home in the morning," Terry explained standing at the foot of her hospital bed.

"Really? I feel like I had brain surgery," Vivian confessed, holding her head between her two hands. "My head is throbbing in a way I can't describe. My vision is a little blurry, too."

"How much do you remember?" Terry inquired.

"About what?" Vivian asked.

"About what happened at the fight?"

"All I remember is being there, cheering and yelling."

"Do you remember who fought?"

Vivian took a few seconds to think about the question-raising her eye brows to deepen her thought, "Simon Davis and some white guy. I don't recall his name. Who came with you?"

"Reggie's waiting in the lobby with that white guy," he told his wife. "His name is Lindsay McKoy. Oh, and Simon won a unanimous decision."

"That's great. I was rooting for him."

"Is that why you were ringside, so you could personally cheer for Simon? Terry inquired.

With a perplexed look on her face, Vivian answered, "Just what do you mean by that exactly?"

"I assumed we had good seats compliments of The Baron," Terry said. "Although, it seems that you weren't satisfied and somehow found your way to Simon Davis' corner. Now, I haven't got a clue as to why you were down there, but I know you can straighten that out for me, right?"

"I don't remember why I was in Davis' corner," Vivian stated. "Besides, my head is killing me. Can you call the nurse? I've been pushing this damn button and they've ignored me."

"Baby, you can't even remember who punched you either?" Terry answered with an angry twinge in his voice.

"No!" Vivian shouted. I don't remember why I was in Davis' corner and I don't know who hit me. The doctors said no one would bother me and that I could rest in peace. Even the police have to hold their questions," Vivian said with tears streaming down her face.

Terry wanted answers but knew he had no other choice but to respect his wife's wishes.

Jaco and the Baron finally arrived to join Reggie in the lobby of the hospital just as Terry exited the elevator.

"So how is she?" The Baron asked with concern.

"Vivian suffered a concussion. Her memory is spotty right now at best," Terry said, his face showing signs of strain from the experience. "I'm going home for a couple of hours to get some sleep. The doctors said Viv can go home in the morning. They want to observe her overnight. I'll be back before they release her."

"Oh, how's my guy, Eddie? Von Mickva asked. "Is he going to be alright?"

"They're still working on him," Reggie said. "He's got a fractured skull, but he's in good hands. I know one of the doctors workin' on him. He'll make it, believe me."

"Eddie worked for me for fourteen years," Von Mickva said. "And . . .well . . .there is nobody in boxing better than Eddie. No one, you hear me? No one."

"I think I'm gonna stick around for a while," Jaco said. "I'll find out how Eddie is doing."

"Yeah, I want know what's going on, too. I'd like to talk to the doctors, myself," Von Mickva said. "Eddie's wife and stepdaughter will probably arrive momentarily and they'll want some answers. What should I tell them?"

"You'll think of something." Reggie said walking towards the main entrance of the hospital.

"Terry, I don't know what to say. I invited you, your wife, and Reggie to the fight. I thought it would be fun but..."

"Look, Baron you couldn't foresee this fiasco, no one could. So don't beat yourself up over it," Terry said.

They gave each other a hug and patted one another on the back, before The Baron suddenly asked, "Why was your wife at ringside?"

Gradually pulling away from Von Mickva, Terry paused a second before answering, "That's a good question."

"Oh, I thought you knew," Von Mickva replied.

"What do you mean exactly?" A vexed Terry inquired.

Terry's question was met with silence, as The Baron, followed by Jaco, walked down the hall and around the corner and then out of sight.

Later that morning, around 11:00 a.m., Reggie and Terry returned to the hospital to pick up Vivian, who was given permission to go home—only if she promised to resume her recuperation there.

Police investigating the incident still weren't given permission to question Vivian because the doctor said she hadn't "regained total recollection of the incident."

Walking gingerly and looking dazed, Vivian exited the hospital on the arm of her husband for the ride to their apartment. Reggie kept photographers at a distance until they sped off.

CHAPTER NINE

A Matter of Deception

Late that night, Terry and Reggie drove upstate to the chateau. The lonesome road was dark and quiet. The moonlight peered through the trees like paparazzi lying in wait for the next sensational scandal. The car was soundless for several miles until Reggie, hands firmly on the steering wheel, suddenly broke the silence.

"It's spooky as hell when neither of us is talking."

Terry waited a moment before speaking, "Oh, I was just thinking about Vivian, hoping she'll be alright."

"She will. Head injuries take a little time to heal, that's all," Reggie said.

"Just hope there is no lingering effects," Terry replied in somber voice.

"Why?" Reggie asked.

"Because Vivian is hard enough to deal with already. I don't need any added vexing," Reggie said.

They both laughed.

"Reggie?"

"Yeah?"

"How are you and your parole officer makin' out?" Terry asked.

"Fine, Just fine."

"Good," Terry said. "I know you were hoping that your P.O. was someone you could work with."

Reggie nodded his head affirming Terry's observation.

"That brings to mind a dream I had two days ago."

"About me?" Reggie asked.

"No. About the Baron, and whether he's someone we should be working with."

"Tell me about it, Man," Reggie said.

"I don't remember the whole thing."

"Well, just tell me what you remember."

"Alright. In my dream, I saw everything going smooth and as planned until we got ready to make our move. Then, all of a sudden, we found out that the Baron wasn't who we thought he was. He was working against us—working with the Fed's," Terry said. "And just like that," Terry warned, smashing his right fist into the palm of his left hand, "we were fucked up, locked down. Finished."

"Well you don't need to worry about the Baron—Jaco either. He's done a lot for people like us in radical situations. He's with us."

"I hope your right."

"I know I'm right," a determined Reggie continued. "Hey, just to make you feel better, I'll have a little chat with him. Besides, if I find out that what you dreamt is true, I'll have no problem lockin' his debonair ass in a room and settin' it on fire."

Terry howled in laughter.

"You know I will" Reggie said, chuckling along with his buddy. "I've done it before and I'll do it again," he added. "They say things are easier the second time around. You see, I went through a lotta shit in prison. The parole board fucked with me because my case was so big in the press and I lingered there, dying inside a little bit every day until they let me out. Soon, those three commissioners on that parole board will have their own hearing—a final hearing and one that will be final indeed."

Terry could see the anger settling in on his best friend's face and the change in the tone of his voice. He felt for him. He knew he was hurting and that he took this situation quite seriously. This is a man whose hatred for the establishment evolved during his stay of incarceration and had now mushroomed into a feverish state of urgency.

Back at the hospital, after six and a half hours of waiting for some answers, the doctor in charge informed the Baron and Jaco that Eddie had sustained a fractured skull induced by repeated blows to the head during the melee that broke out at the Felt Forum.

Eddie's skull was repaired in surgery and, the doctor said, he would be able to resume training fighters in time. The Baron expressed joy over the news and promised to grant his prized trainer all the time he needed to recuperate.

Von Mickva had never considered another man to train his fighters. Training fighters was Eddie's expertise, which made him so valuable to the Baron. Eddie had laced up the gloves of seventeen champions in six weight classes over a forty year career—fourteen of them with the Baron.

"How was Minnesota?" Terry asked.

"It's was pretty interesting," Reggie answered with a laugh.

"Yeah? How so?"

"Well, for one thing, Jaco is a very resourceful motherfucker," Reggie said. "By the way, Terry, what happened to the Pavulon we had at the chateau?" he asked, countering with a question of his own.

"I don't know. I think one of the workers at the house stole that shit, not knowing what it was," Terry said.

"Yeah, well I hope he uses it and dies—the bastard."

Reggie and Terry chuckled, but Terry laughed so hard he almost choked.

"Oh, he'll die if he uses that shit, believe me," Terry said as he tried to clear his throat. "But, tell me about Minnesota."

"Oh yeah," Reggie continued. "As soon as we got to Minnesota we went to a hospital where Jaco knew this woman, a Dr. Yogami. He had a past relationship with her that was serious enough that he was planning to marry her. She also happens to run the pharmaceutical department."

"Wait a minute," Terry said. "Let me get this straight. You mean to tell me that Jaco knows a doctor—a drug doctor?"

"What did I say?" Reggie asked, smirking. "We waited until the late shift. That's when Jaco went into her office and had some private time with the Doc. You know what I mean? I waited until he got her nice and preoccupied, then wearing a lab coat, I snuck into Dr. Yogami's office, passed the two of them, and into the pharmaceutical supply room next to her office. That's where they keep the Pavulon. I had to get it, man, 'cause that was the whole point of the trip."

Terry was speechless, but not totally surprised by Jaco's unwavering determination. He saw a problem—no Pavulon—and he solved it, simple as that.

Terry thought about how Vivian would've reacted also if he had gone on the trip to Minnesota with Reggie and Jaco. She would have pitched a fit, that's for sure. Maybe Jaco is the right man for this job. But it was the Baron's motives that Terry wasn't so certain about.

After dropping off the Pavulon at the chateau, Reggie and Terry headed back to New York City. A seemingly uneventful foray turned dreadfully unpredictable when a New York State highway trooper ordered them to pullover while driving through Poughkeepsie.

"Stay cool, it's only one trooper," Terry reminded Reggie.

"You mean you don't want me to wack him?" Reggie replied sarcastically, looking through the rear view mirror to gauge the trooper's location.

"May I see your license and registration?" the trooper asked.

Reggie remained motionless, lips tightened, maintaining a constant grip on the steering wheel. He utterly loathed law enforcement and everything it stands for. He hated the stress it had put upon his family and his own life.

"Hey!" the trooper shouted, "Did you hear me? I need to see your license and registration!"

A dual exchange took place. Reggie reached for his wallet. The trooper reached for his gun.

"Damn, your ass is tight to shoot somebody," Reggie said handing his wallet over to the trooper.

Remaining silent, the trooper inspected the license.

"Get out of the fucking car and open the damn trunk!" the trooper yelled at Reggie suddenly.

Reggie wanted to flip out. Instead, he held his composure, reminding himself of the big picture.

"Open it now!" the trooper repeated.

The trunk popped open revealing two 9 millimeter handguns, neatly displayed as if being auctioned off at Sotheby's.

"Put your hands up nigger," the trooper ordered pointing his gun at Reggie's head. "As soon as I stopped you I knew you were dirty."

Terry leaped from the car and charged in the direction of the trunk.

"What's going on officer?"

"Don't take another step, asshole," the trooper said pointing his gun at Terry.

With vile bitterness, the trooper spilled the entire contents of Reggie's wallet onto the asphalt and handcuffed Reggie.

Suddenly, a second trooper's car veered abruptly to a halt.

"What's going on here?" asked the second trooper, whose dull blue shirt displayed two gold bars on the collar, tagging him as a lieutenant.

"Oh, lieutenant...I got one with two nines," the first trooper answered.

The lieutenant looked both men over then asked, "Did you check to see if he has a permit for those weapons?"

"Uh, no. I-I was gonna do that at the station house," the trooper nervously answered.

"Do it now," the lieutenant ordered, standing with his hands on his hips, legs spread apart.

The trooper began to sort through the items strewn about the pavement until he found something. Holding it in his hand, he stood up and faced the lieutenant.

"What'cha got?" the lieutenant asked.

"Permits, sir...for both of 'em."

"And are they valid?"

"Yeah."

"Well then uncuff the man," demanded the lieutenant, pointing his index finger at Reggie's manacled hands.

In the moments subsequent to his liberation, Reggie saw the paradox of it all. Here were two men: One white trooper, who wished to treat him as his forefathers had in the past; and the other, a black lieutenant who wanted to protect his civil rights. What a world.

Driving away with the distance between the troopers and themselves increasing, Terry couldn't help but think about the propensity for volatility they had left behind. Had it not been for that lieutenant, they would've found themselves mere prey for a racist trooper's maniacal rage.

Terry and Reggie talked about their seemingly close call as they headed downstate towards New York City. It was then, near the Peekskill County line, that Reggie again noticed a state trooper's car in close pursuit. Once the trooper's car approached, Reggie smiled delightfully surprised.

"Mr. Cochran, when are you going to start obeying the laws of this state?" the lieutenant from the previous encounter asked.

"As soon as you stop masquerading as a lieutenant trooper, Jaco," Reggie said.

Smiling with his hands folded and tucked against his chest Jaco asked, "You knew it was me?"

"Hell yeah," added Reggie, "Not many black troopers in this hillbilly part of New York—let alone a black lieutenant looking out for my rights."

"Well I guess I played it up a little too much, huh?" Jaco asked.

"You had me fooled," Terry confessed. "I called Jaco on the cell phone," Terry said, "but I had no idea he would come dressed like a fuckin' state trooper lieutenant."

"So, Terry...you called him, huh?"

"Yup. While that asshole was rousting you."

"When that trooper-that dumb ass that he is—finds out that my being a lieutenant was nothing but a ruse...he's gonna feel like such an ass."

"A complete jackass," Reggie said. "Hey, by the way, how did you get that uniform and the car, Jaco?"

"If I tell you that you wouldn't need me on your team," Jaco said laughing. "Now get outta here before I lock you up for real."

Reggie checked his watch, suddenly remembering the pressing need to get to the city. The two old friends quickly got back on the road.

Meanwhile, back in Manhattan, Vivian began shaking off the effects of her concussion and started resuming her normal activities. She attended to her personal errands, took long walks and went on shopping jaunts. It was on one of those jaunts that Vivian inadvertently ran into Simon Davis outside a swanky Fifth Avenue boutique.

She pretended as though her interest in Simon was purely as a boxing fan. After all, Simon held the title of heavyweight champ of the World Boxing Council. But her curiosity about him was more of a personal nature.

As they walked together, poking in and out of fashionable stores, Simon began to notice that Vivian had indeed felt a physical attraction towards him. Evidenced by her asking questions like: "Do you think I could hold your attention wearing this?" as they stood staring through the window of a lingerie store.

Simon felt somewhat uncomfortable attempting to get closer to Vivian, despite her flirtatious advances. He was clearly aware of the fact that she was a married woman. All that changed at a cozy bistro when Vivian confided that the revitalized relationship between her husband, Terry and Reggie Cochran left their marriage broken and her sex life literally unfulfilled.

She hinted at her willingness to accept the shattered union, but also indicated that she couldn't bear a neglected sex life. Simon believed Vivian's confessions, especially as he became mesmerized by the flecks of gold in her brown eyes and the way she threw her head back whenever she laughed. Under the soft lights and after enjoying the good meal he had treated her to, he was more than willing to fill her sexual void. An affair ensued.

It started that afternoon in a Lexington Avenue hotel. Soon they moved their trysts to the Vernon, New Jersey home Vivian shared with her husband. Vivian didn't care. Simon was great for her, a muscle-bound Casanova who created the much needed electricity and sexual fulfillment Vivian desperately desired in her life.

Meanwhile, Reggie was frustrated. Trying to find a parking space on a Saturday at Aqueduct Raceway was like trying to find a water fountain in the Mojave Desert. But this was no ordinary Saturday afternoon at the races. The running of the Wood Memorial, a graded stakes race, was the highlight of the day.

In Reggie's opinion, this was a strange place to meet the Baron about the operation. But he needed to make Terry feel comfortable with the mission. And the only way to do that was to get some definitive answers to Terry's questions about the Baron and the F.B.I.

After making his way into the raceway, Reggie's senses were struck by the blend of fast foods, beer and cigar and cigarette smoke. He estimated that the crowd was made up of about three fifths senior citizens and two fifths young- and middle-aged adults.

The atmosphere reminded Reggie of the stock market. Just like investors, horse players were huddled in small groups, some stood alone, and everyone was busy analyzing statistical information about the horses' past races, breeding, speed figures, inclination towards turf as opposed to grass, whether the horse is early or late runner and other highly technical information needed to pick a winner.

Even after the players chose the horse they would bet on, they continued checking their calculations while frantically heading towards multiple automated betting counters to place their bets. Some of the gamblers seemed a bit hesitant about placing their bets, but most left the counters appearing optimistic that their bets would return a profit.

Reggie sliced through the crowd to find a spot where he could watch the race. He didn't want to see it on the monitors inside the arena. He wanted to take in the full ambiance of the beautifully manicured racetrack, gleaming horses and impeccably dressed jockeys. Reggie even admired the artistic landscaping of flowers positioned to highlight the design of the track.

"Did you drop this, Sugar?" asked an attractive auburn-haired woman who was bending down to pick up something from the floor.

"That's my ticket," Reggie said. "Thanks. I didn't realize I had dropped it."

"Yeah, well you did. I've been watchin' you for the last five minutes," she replied as she handed Reggie the ticket.

Reggie watched her as she walked away. Her short denim mini skirt didn't leave much to the imagination. And her ravishingly long legs were two of the three reasons Reggie kept his eye on this woman. He took note as she walked past the Baron on her way to her seat in an area designated for VIPs. The Baron also stopped to watch her walk even though he had been chatting with three dark-suited men, all wearing sunglasses.

In contrast to his typical leadership presence, the powerful Baron—a terrorism deal maker, a boxing promoter of champions, and an international jet-setter worth millions of dollars—seemed humbled, subservient and almost child-like as he stood before the three men. They talked and he listened. Reggie wondered who they were and what hold they had on Von Mivkva. But before Reggie could put the puzzle together, the men abruptly left and the Baron headed to his seat.

"Hey, Baron," Reggie said as he approached. "With all these people here I didn't expect to find you so quickly."

"Hey, Reggie! I'm glad you could come," the Baron said. "Come on over. Have a seat. Isn't this a great day for a horse race?"

"Yes it is. I didn't know you liked the races. What brings you out here to the racetrack?"

"Actually, PhotoFinish brought me here," the Baron said.

"Come again?"

"My horse, PhotoFinish, is the reason I'm here today. A business associate owed me more money than he could afford to pay. So, what do you give the man who has everything? An all-expense paid trip around the world? Nah. A million dollar marker for the tables in Vegas? How 'bout a brand spanking new John Deere power mower to make you feel like a man? Bullshit. Picture this...I'm at this bastard's house—a sprawling ranch house in Kentucky. So, I say to this asshole, 'I'll take one of those racehorses you got in the barn.' He ranted and raved. Talking about this is my livelihood, di-da-di-dadi-da. You know what I said, Reggie?"

"No. What?"

"I told him that if he didn't give me that horse he would have no fucking horse farm. So that's how I got the racehorse," he explained laughing.

"That's a touching story, Baron," Reggie said, laughing. As he composed himself, he turned to the Baron.

"Hey, would you answer one question for me?"

"Yeah, sure," the Baron said. "What's on your mind?"

"I don't mean to pry but, who were those three guys you were talking to before I came over?"

"You saw me talking to those guys?" the Baron asked, scratching the back of his neck.

"Yeah."

"Those gentlemen are carrying out some functions for me," the Baron said. "And that's all I'm going to say about the matter."

Reggie wondered whether the Baron was being truthful. "I've got a lot riding on my plans, you know," he said, his eyes bulging wide.

"Yes of course," the Baron stressed. "But I'll have you know that I wouldn't have dropped $4.6 million on you if I didn't believe in you. Believing in you means getting on that surfboard and riding out those waves. Do you understand?"

"Because I don't need the F.B..."

"You think those gentleman are F.B.I.?" the Baron said interrupting Reggie.

"I-I wasn't sure. As soon as I saw them I started feeling funny."

"Funny like how, Reggie. Funny like how?"

"Like the feeling you get when you start to realize that you might be getting set up by an F.B.I. informant in a sting operation."

"Reggie, listen," Von Mickva said. "You know I'm a double-edged sword. On one hand, I have a public image with boxing and my other businesses. On the other hand, I have a dark side—my gray area—and I don't need the government in my affairs."

The seventh race ended with the favorite, Knight Force, winning his third straight allowance race. My Baby came in second for a 3-7 exacta that returned $22.60.

Reggie received a call on his seldom-used cell phone and abruptly rose from his seat.

"You're leaving? Von Mickva queried. "My horse runs next. You'll be insulting me if you don't stay."

"Sorry. I gotta meet someone."

When Reggie reached about twenty feet away he heard the Baron call to him. "Hey, Reggie, yesterday you called me wanting to talk about something."

"We already did," Reggie replied, waving his hand and rushing off.

Despite the heat and haziness of the afternoon, Paulino's, a quaint, bustling, Italian restaurant tucked away in Manhattan's theater district, ensured its patrons were kept happy by providing unending hospitality and cool air conditioned comfort. The restaurant's dimly lit dining room, complimented by the Sinatra-like vocal stylings of Jimmy Rosselli and the authentic Italian cuisine, made Paulino's a favorite of New Yorkers and tourists from the world over.

Terry had been occupying the same back table, the one against the wall and facing the window, every Saturday evening for the last two years. He was enjoying his favorite dish on Paulino's menu, baked ziti with marinara sauce while he waited for Reggie to arrive.

"Look at you," Reggie said when he finally arrived, "Stuffing your face! What's this-a ritual?"

"You know me and Saturday nights. It's Paulino's," Terry said, banging his fist on the table. "Why are you so late, man?"

"Traffic. It was bumper to bumper coming from Aqueduct. I got here as quickly as I could," Reggie explained.

"Can I get you something?" the waiter asked.

"Aaahhh, just a double Jim Bean on the rocks," Reggie ordered.

"And how is your ziti, Mr. Williams...to your satisfaction?" the waiter asked Terry.

"Scrumptious. No other word could describe it."

"Good. I know the manager will be pleased," the waiter said before walking off to fetch the Jim Bean.

"You met with the Baron?" Terry asked in between morsels.

"Yup."

"Well, what did he say?"

"About what?"

"The dream I told you about. The one about the Baron and the F.B.I."

"Oh yeah. He said he wasn't involved with the F.B.I., but that's not the strange part."

"What happened?"

"Well when I went to see him at Aqueduct...I noticed that he was in deep conversation with these men—three men to be exact—and they were all dressed in black."

"Who were they?"

"Beats me, Terry, but it looks to me like the Baron was obligated to those men or whomever they represent. I was really concerned that they might have some kind of leverage over him."

"I knew it!" Terry shouted, causing heads to turn in the quiet restaurant. "What did I tell you? I knew it," he whispered.

"No, Terry. You had a dream. You told me about your dream, man. Seems that I have partially confirmed it, but I still have to do more checking to know for sure."

"Yeah, but you would've never began to check if it hadn't been for me. And you know that."

"That's true," Reggie answered reluctantly, scratching the left side of his face.

"Any ideas on how we can be 100 percent sure?

"Skip Raymond is an ex-F.B.I counter-intelligence agent. He was locked up with me in Comstock on a check forgery conviction. All he did was spy on people, eavesdropping, surveillance and all that. I'll give him a call. He could probably help," Reggie said.

It took Reggie five tries over the course of a week and a half before he reached the elusive Skip Raymond on the phone at his Park Slope, Brooklyn home. He invited Reggie over the following day.

When he arrived, Reggie wasn't prepared for what he saw. Dirty socks and other personal articles were strewn about the floor. Used coffee cups were mingled with unwashed spaghetti sauce pots in the sink. Empty liquor bottles and shot glasses poked out from under the bed, telling Reggie that his old buddy was in bad shape when it came to alcohol.

Despite the crime scene-like atmosphere, Skip received Reggie with open arms. The two former cell mates hadn't set eyes on each other since their prison days.

Skip admitted to Reggie that he had somewhat of a hard time adjusting to life after being released from prison in 1995. His wife had divorced him, which he confessed was not a shock. But he was very surprised that he couldn't find work anywhere, which he attributed to the F.B.I. Skip figured that the agency must have put the word out in the security and private investigation community. He admitted that it was the only work he knew. He had entered the bureau when he was only 22 years old. After they caught up on each other's lives, Skip abruptly changed the subject.

"You're not here to hear my sad story, man. What can I do for you, Reggie?"

Holding back his thoughts, Reggie began tapping his fingers on a side table positioned next to the couch.

"Stop doing that would you please?" Skip said, obviously irritated by the noise.

"It's bothering you?" Reggie said in a probing tone.

"Yeah. It bothers me. Do you mind? I got problems here."

"Sure, Skip. I'll stop if it bothers you."

"It bothers me, Reggie. It bothers me."

"Alright," Reggie said with a tinge of anger in his voice. "You ain't the only one with problems."

"I know, man. "So what's up?"

Reggie stood up and began pacing from left to right. "I got problems, Skip. Big problems."

"So how can I help?" Skip said, almost pleading with his friend.

"You still know how to do that surveillance stuff, eavesdropping and all that shit?"

"Yeah. Of course. You don't forget that kinda shit."

"Good. I need to know about a guy."

Skip, the pot-bellied, silver-haired former investigator reached for a cigarette and lit it.

"Who is he?" Skip asked.

"He's a British Baron. His name is Baron Von Mickva. He has homes in London and Las Vegas and rents in New York. He's a promoter and manager of professional boxers and he owns a thoroughbred race horse. But the Baron's loves investing in unique events."

"What are you working on?" Skip asked.

"It's the operation of all operations. A remedy for which there is no accord. Does that answer your question?"

With a broad grin and a quiet laugh, Skip replied, "Nope, you gotta tell me more than that."

"The ten years I spent in prison. All those wasted years. The loss of my dreams and all the shit I had to take from those bastards C.O.s. Have you heard enough yet?"

"Yeah," replied Skip, putting his cigarette out in the ashtray. "I'll do it. How much will you pay me?"

"Does $10,000.00 sound good to you?"

"Fuckin'-A. Not that I need it or anything." Skip said smiling.

"Yeah, right," Reggie said chuckling.

Skip Raymond had no problem getting to know his subject. It seemed that everything Baron Von Mickva did attracted the media like a magnet.

Within a week of Reggie giving him the assignment Skip found himself attending the Bi-Coastal Boxing Writers Association Awards Dinner at the Grand Hyatt Hotel, where the Baron was recipient of their "Lifetime Contributor to The Sport of Boxing Award".

After the affair the Baron shook hands with well-wishers and made his way to his Rolls Royce.

"Baron!" A voice from the crowd called out as he was about to pull off.

"Jaco, get in," the Baron said. "Can I drop you off somewhere?"

"I thought we might talk."

"Not now. I'm very tired. Besides, I have some important meetings tomorrow," Von Mickva said through a yawn."

"What's eating you?"

"Nothing I can't handle my friend. Nothing I can't handle," the Baron said as he rubbed his palms together.

"Bullshit."

"What did you just say to me?"

"Baron, I mean no disrespect, but we've done it all together. Everything. Ev-ery-thing. And now, after all these years, you wanna shut me out?"

As the burgundy British luxury vehicle swerved along Broadway, the Baron sighed deeply and began mumbling to himself. It sounded to Jaco that he was saying that he couldn't let the proverbial cat out of the bag.

It was true that Jaco had been involved in several dark endeavors with the Baron and that the two old friends shared a multitude of dark secrets. However, Von Mickva felt strongly that he had an inalienable right to decide issues related to his freedom without the inclusion of Jaco. Otherwise, those decisions would become a small-scale quorum, and Jaco would have to share the blame for the outcome.

"As close as we are and as much as we've been through together, it hurts me that you feel I'm shutting you out," the Baron said.

"Well, you should walk in my shoes."

"I have—many, many times. That's why I'm striving with every fiber in my being to protect you, old boy."

"Protect me? From what?"

"The bureaucratic wickedness designed to deter your career," Von Mickva replied matter-of-factly.

"What the fuck are you talking about?"

"Oh, wake up, man. We occupy a gray area of society, outside the margins, so to speak. What we do is not a Fortune 500 occupation. We do what we do and that's it. We're outta there."

"I don't get it," said Jaco. "I just don't get it."

Von Mickva instructed his driver to stop the car in front of a non-descript apartment building on 91st Street and Columbus Avenue.

"How did you know I was going here?" Jaco asked before he exited the car.

"Because that's where the girls are, my boy. You forgot I dropped you off here before."

Jaco noticed that it was unusually quiet on the block. Typically, early morning stragglers could be seen returning from after-hour nightclubs or elsewhere. Occasionally, Jaco would hear a couple arguing in the wee hours of the morning, too. He wasn't sure why today was so different, but he stepped into the vestibule and pressed the intercom button above the nameplate that read Prescott Travel, Inc. No vacations were ever booked at this residence. It was exactly the way the Baron had described it. This place was "where the girls are."

"Who's there?" an older woman with a raspy voice spoke through the box.

"It's me, Jaco."

"Who?"

"Jaco. You gonna let me in?"

The door clicked open.

Upstairs on the second floor, two beautifully statuesque women stood in the doorway both wearing only their panties and bras.

"Jaco, where the hell you been? We've missed you."

"Ladies, ladies. I missed you, too. But I've been busy on the road.

"We go through withdrawal, Jaco when you don't come by often," purred the blonde as she massaged her grapefruit-sized breasts.

"Yeah, Baby," affirmed the brunette.

"Every time I leave here you ladies leave me drained. If I stopped by every night my thighs would shrink down to the size of two cigarettes."

"Come in and shut the door!" said the woman with the raspy voice from inside the apartment.

The place was familiar to Jaco. He had been a patron for years. The spacious living room was decorated with seven other attractive, scantily-clad women draped over two black leather sofas. Bargain store paintings adorned the walls and a round glass cocktail table separated the two sofas.

The carpet was several shades darker than the original green it had been. An untold number of impatient tricks eager to get their hump on had either paced that carpet beyond recognition as they waited for their favorite girl or had simply stomped out their cigarettes on the carpet in the rush to get behind closed doors with any working girl.

This agency wasn't on the level of those run by upscale Manhattan madams. This was prostitution in a brown paper bag. Here, the word escort does not prefix service. This was service only. The proprietor, Sally Ruffo, was a portly, raspy-voiced, foul-mouthed, middle-aged woman with an arrest record dating back to 1971.

Sally ran a tight ship. You weren't going to find any of her girls standing on street corners or hanging around dark hotels and motels throughout the city. They did their work in-house in plain sight of Ruffo. The girls understood the rules and they were paid adequately.

Lela, the blonde and Lotus Blossom, the brunette, were making a beeline towards one of the back bedrooms to accommodate Jaco before they were stopped by Sally.

"How long you been comin' here, Jaco?" Sally asked.

"About six years. Why?"

"Have any one of my girls ever treated you badly when you visit?"

"No. Why do you ask?"

"Because you rang my bell, talked to Lela and Lotus Blossom outside the door, and now you think you're gonna high-tail it to one of my rooms, while all the time forgetting to do the most important thing."

"What?" Jaco asked.

"Muthafuka, you forgot to say hello to me and the rest of my girls, you asshole!"

"Oh, shit! I'm sorry, Sally. How are you and the girls? How's tricks?"

Sally tightened her lips and narrowed her eyes, "You're a jackass. You know that? Get out of here. Fuck or get your dick sucked or whatever you do back there."

Jaco wondered if Sally had all her wits about her. For the past six years he had tolerated her incessant barking and snarling about this and that. Jaco would gladly underwrite her attendance in psychotherapy, however he had no real confidence that she would ever attend sessions. Jaco was convinced that a multitude of issues lay buried beneath the surface of Sally's psyche—a repressed childhood, a low self-esteem, a case of domestic abuse and overwhelming guilt and responsibility for four failed marriages.

Jaco even contemplated scouring the city for another hangout, but once he got to the back room at Sally's all those thoughts perished.

Meanwhile, nearly two weeks had elapsed before Skip contacted Reggie at the Cottenwood. He and Terry were watching a video when the call came in.

"You mean you knew this guy instigated revolutions in foreign governments?"

Reggie and Terry answered harmoniously,

"Yes."

"And you never said nothing?"

"That's beside the point," Reggie said.

"What would you say his frame of mind is right now?" Terry probed.

"Facing the possibility of a long prison term, disgrace and embarrassment, I'm guessing that the Baron is leaning towards offering up some juicy lyrics if the government would drop the charges their holding against him."

"What kind of juicy lyrics?" Reggie asked.

"Based on what I've seen, I'd say Baron Von Mickva is about to sleep with the enemy," Skip said.

CHAPTER TEN

And The New Heavyweight Champion of the World...

'We must have been sadists,' Reggie thought, remembering his and Terry's attendance the week prior at Madison Square Garden for the eastern conference semifinal playoff game. The Knicks were walloped by the Indiana Pacers by twenty seven points at that game.

Terry decided to accompany Reggie to his Cottenwood digs in the Bronx after stopping at a few of his favorite watering holes.

He was quite aware that his decision to dock and lodge at Reggie's place would draw the ire of Vivian, but he didn't care. Lately, he had been finding reasons to stay away from their Rockland County home. He had made a pact with himself to assist Reggie and to see his operation through until the end.

They both worked deep into the wee hours of the morning discussing strategy, tactics and logistics that would ensure the success of such a brazen undertaking.

The doorbell rang and both Reggie and Terry jumped up to see who was calling. The two old friends were seemingly on edge as a result of the dynamics of their intense planning session.

Sylvia Mitchell stood at the door wearing her signature aren't-you-thrilled-to-see-me expression. Her white mini-skirt was soaking wet and her black knee-high boots were soiled with clumps of mud from the thunderstorm.

"Sylvia, what are you doing out in the storm?" Reggie asked.

"I came to see you, Silly," Sylvia said as she slid her soggy hair from in front of her face. "Can I come in?"

"Oh-oh, sure. Come in."

Sylvia sashayed down the foyer, her waterlogged boots squeaking like a tracking device. She stopped at the entrance to the kitchen where Terry was standing.

"Well, aren't you going to say hello?"

"I don't talk to tailgaters," Terry replied.

"What did I do, Terry? Exactly what did I do?"

"Don't fuck with me, Terry said, glaring at Sylvia. "You know what you did."

"I'm not in the mood to play games," she said moving her wet face to just inches away from his. "You got something to say to me? Let's hear it."

Terry lost his head and slapped her with the back of his hand. Sylvia spun around from the force and fell into Reggie's extended arms. Terry moved quickly towards her.

"Don't you ever follow me to Menands or anywhere else—ever!" he yelled, pointing his finger directly in her face.

"Okay. Okay," said Sylvia sobbing. I didn't know I was doing anything wrong. I didn't mean to. You've got to believe me."

Reggie eventually got Terry to calm down-explaining to him that Sylvia had nothing to gain from following him. She hadn't broken any laws and had never met Baron Von Mickva.

Terry thought about Reggie's summary for about a minute or two and decided he was right.

"Hell, no harm. No foul," he said, waving his hand toward Sylvia.

"Can I take off my boots?" Sylvia asked, hoping to change the subject. "They're so wet."

Reggie led her to the bathroom, plucking his bathrobe out of the closet on the way.

"Here, put this on. That micro-skirt is sticking to your body. I can even see the color of your panties."

"No, you can't!" Sylvia shot back.

"Oh, yeah? How you gonna tell me what I can see or not?"

"Because, I'm not wearing any panties. That's how I know," she said, peeling out of her wet mini to substantiate her declaration.

"Wow! I'll see you after you freshen up," Reggie said, walking out of the room backwards.

"What am I gonna do with that lady?" he asked Terry when he returned to the living room. "I'm surprised she came here after the argument we had at the Felt Forum."

"Yeah? What did you two argue about?"

"She was pissed that I didn't keep in touch with her after we slept together."

"Well, you know how it is, man. Women are like that," Terry said.

"I know but I had a good reason."

"Yeah, what was it?"

"She slept with me while her husband and children were in the house."

"Get the fuck out of here."

"I bullshit you not."

"You never told me Sylvia fucked you while her husband and kids were home."

"Yup. That bitch is crazy."

"Crazy is putting it mildly, my friend."

"Anyway, what were we talking about earlier?" Reggie continued. "We're not gonna be able to stay here after this shit is over."

"Where you wanna go?"

"Maybe Bhutan, Western Sahara, Dubai, Kazakhstan or Croatia. There's no extradition treaty with the U.S. in any of those countries."

"Reggieeeee," Sylvia purred from the bedroom.

"What?"

"Come here," She sang out.

"Oh, boy. I know what she wants."

"She still loves you."

"Reggieeeee," Sylvia called again. "Come on. I wanted to show you something."

"What do you want to show me, Sylvia?" Reggie asked, leaning against the frame of the bedroom door.

Sylvia strolled over gingerly but stopped about a foot in front of Reggie. She gently slid the robe off her shoulders to reveal a honey-toned, finely-chiseled voluptuous body.

"You wanna peak at this?"

"What's your husband gonna say?"

"Nothing. I left him months ago. The divorce will be final in another week or so," she said with a smirk. "It's one of those quickie divorces, you know," she began unbuckling his belt.

"Where are the kids?"

"They're with my mother. I like a man who's concerned about my kids," she purred. "Look, Babe, I'm sorry about before, I should have told you that my family was home. Again, I'm sorry," she said, unbuttoning Reggie's shirt.

"Reggie picked her up in his arms and placed her on his bed.

"So, you wanted to fuck?"

"Absolutely," she said, smiling.

"You sound like you're confessing."

"Shut up and put it in me Mr. Man," she swooned.

The howl of raw sex reverberating throughout the apartment reminded Terry of the hump sessions he and Vivian used to enjoy when times were better. Reggie and Sylvia had been at it for at least an hour and a half. Terry assumed they'd be tired by now. But orgasm-building must have recharged their batteries because they continued. Terry wished his batteries were as durable.

He wandered into the kitchen and made himself a turkey and Swiss cheese sandwich. Finding two beers in the fridge, Terry drank them both, knowing Reggie wouldn't mind—especially since he wasn't getting what Reggie was getting right now. It seemed like a reasonable concession.

"Why did you come here, Sylvia?"

"I told you. I wanted to see you," she said, rolling over on her stomach and stroking Reggie's hairy chest.

"That might be part of it. But why did you really come here?"

Sylvia's eyes welled up with emotion. "I still love you, Reg."

"Oh, please," he said, his eyebrows furrowed with suspicion.

"And I know you still love..."

"Of course, I still love you," he said interrupting her. "I did then and I do now, but what does that mean?"

"It means that despite our past problems and misunderstandings we could make it work this time. What I'm trying to say is...let's get married again, Reggie. Huh, whatdaya' say?"

Reggie respectfully declined. He took his time explaining that his life was entirely too complex right now for a relationship—let alone a marriage. But Sylvia kept the pressure up for two whole hours. Reggie was unyielding. She simply couldn't change his mind. Still, Sylvia held out for the possibility that with the right choice of words and conviction Reggie would see that a relationship renewal was feasible.

All of a sudden the bedroom door swung open.

"Damn, Terry, knock next time! Can't you see I'm not dressed?" Sylvia snapped.

"I wasn't looking, but since I know how you feel, I'll be sure to bring my camera next time."

"Never mind her. What's going on?" Reggie asked.

"Skip just called. He wants us to meet him outside the U.S. Attorney's office."

It took Terry and Reggie forty-five minutes to reach the U.S. Attorney's Office for the Southern District in New York. The office was located in lower Manhattan.

Scanning the block looking for Skip, they soon noticed his used Toyota Celica parked in the middle of the block.

"So, what's up?" Reggie asked.

"He's been in there for at least an hour," Skip informed Reggie and Terry between rapid drags of a cigarette.

"Can we listen in?" Terry inquired, "You said you had mic'd his clothing."

"I put listening devices in five of his suits," Skip said. "He must be wearing a new one. I'm not getting any signal." Skip pointed to a briefcase next to him that should have been receiving a signal from the planted device.

Silence replaced their peaked anticipation that would actually hear the Baron ratting on their operation.

"You guys kinda look tired-no sleep last night?" Skip asked.

"Not me!" Terry answered quickly. "It's Reggie. He's the one who fucked all morning.

"Fuck you!" Reggie said.

Skip and Terry busted into laughter.

"I used to bust yo' ass when we were kids...don't make me do it again, alright?"

"You see, you see, how sensitive he gets, Skip?"

"Don't put me in that shit," Skip said blowing smoke out of both his mouth and nose at once.

"I was only joking, man. Damn."

"Well, don't joke like that. That's my business...we ain't down here for all that," Reggie said.

"Got any ideas?" Terry asked.

"Good question," Reggie said. "What's an honorable way for a noble snitch to die? Let me count the ways," Reggie joked. "One, that fancy Rolls Royce of his could be custom-fitted with high-impact explosives set to go off whenever I want it to. Two, it could be done in a low-key sort of way-by virtue of the poisoning of his favorite dish. Three, a fire could breakout in his hotel room and melt Von Mickva's big mouth shut. Four, there could be an invasion of that same hotel room by masked intruders hyped to blow his disloyal brains out.

"Reggie."

Looking up, Reggie said, "What's on your mind Skip?"

"I've been thinking, man. I've been doing this work for you and it's cool," he said. "This shit's got my engine revved up like the old days with the Bureau. But I want more. I need more. Hell, you gettin' ready to commit the crime of the century. Whatever happens, good or bad, they'll never forget you."

Terry and Reggie smiled at each other. They both opted to remain silent while Skip continued his speech.

"A divorce, unemployment, losing the house that I've lived in for the last nineteen years..." Skip said. "There's nothing positive left for me. No sunshine peering through my window. I guess what I'm trying to say is..."

"What you're trying to say, Skip, is that you want in. You wanna be part of the team 'til the end. Do I hear you correctly?" Reggie asked.

"Damn right you do," Skip replied, holding his head and cigarette up proudly.

"You understand that from this moment on it's gonna be dangerous, crazy and over the top."

Skip nodded.

"Skip, I hope you're not doing this for your own self-serving reasons—a sort of stick-it-to-the-state-so-the-feds-will-listen kinda thing?"

"Absolutely not!" Skip said firmly.

"Cuz if that's it, I'm okay with it," Reggie said. "I don't give a fuck as long as the mission gets done."

All three men shook on it. Having Skip, an ex-FBI agent, on the team would only enhance their objective—making a complicated task more doable.

"Three more guys," Reggie said cryptically.

"I don't understand."

"Skip, I need three more guys."

"Oh, why didn't you say so? I would've offered, only I didn't feel it was my place. You understand."

"You know some people?" Terry asked

"Yes. I know precisely the three guys you need. They were a mere oversight for the FBI's Ten Most Wanted List before I left the Bureau. I met them under dubious circumstances. You understand?"

"They sound like they've got the right pedigree," Terry said.

"They're the best," Skip admitted.

"Good. When can we meet them?"

"Let me get in touch with them. I know they'll do it. That shit is right up their alley. We'll set up a meeting."

Upstairs in the office of assistant U.S. Attorney Strobe Nix, Baron Von Mickva was not completely sold on the idea of, in Strobe's words, "Coming into camp."

Nix made it clear that his promise of no jail time, a million dollar fine and five months house arrest stood firm against the Baron's imminent federal indictment and likely conviction. The Baron's massive legal problems were in connection with his financial involvement in the conspiracy to support Islamic fundamentalist in plots to overthrow the

Yemen and Iranian governments in exchange for information leading to the arrest, indictment and conviction of the person or persons who had or were about to commit criminal acts against local, state and the federal government.

It was a lofty promise. A necessary overture to procure the unyielding cooperation of a central figure, who when flipped would reveal where all the proverbial bodies were buried. But there was one hitch. In order for a deal between Von Mickva and the U.S. Attorney's office to be consummated, the Baron would have to talk, name names and give details. And he hadn't intended on doing any of that-certainly not without a lawyer present.

Terry suddenly had an idea. He and Reggie hopped out of Skip's car to make a telephone call. The two of them, at the insistence of Terry, rode to his home in Vernon, New Jersey to pick up some clothes. Terry wanted to tell Vivian that he loved her, despite his ignoring her constant demands that he sever his relationship with Reggie. Still, it was clear to Terry that their marriage was finished.

Upon entering the house, Terry heard moans, groans and sighs coming from the bedroom. He opened the door to find Vivian in bed with none other than Simon Davis. They were so involved in their sexual activity-clinching, holding, kissing and sucking that it took more than twenty seconds before they realized Terry had caught them in the act.

"Oh, shit! Terry! How long you been standing there?" Vivian asked, quickly pulling the sheets up around her body.

Staring at her with the eyes of a maniac, Terry replied, "Long enough. Be right back," Terry said, bolting from the bedroom door and running wildly down the hallway. Terry found a halogen floor lamp and ripped it from the socket. He immediately returned to the bedroom.

"Hey-hey, Terry," Simon began to plead. "I'm outta here," Simon said while grabbing his clothing, which had been strewn about the room. "I don't want no trouble," he added.

Vivian leaped off the bed and hunkered down in the corner of the room, her knees tucked under her chin. She began to cry into her hands. She had never seen that look in Terry's eyes before and could predict what he was about to do.

Terry began brutally attacking Simon with the floor lamp. Although, Simon begged Terry to stop, he continued until the lamp broke in half and lodged itself in a window on the other side of the room. He resumed the beating with his right foot, kicking Simon about the head and chest until blood began to flow.

"You're gonna kill him if you keep kicking him like that!" Vivian cried out.

"What, bitch?" Terry screamed as he bolted over to her.

Terry's two hands were suddenly around Vivian's throat.

"Don't you know that I will kill you outright?" he seethed, sweat dripping from his forehead and chin. "This muthafucker lying bloody and busted up is yo' damn fault. Now I understand why you were ringside at the Davis fight."

Vivian wanted to beg for her life but couldn't mouth the words as Terry progressively tightened his grip around her neck.

"Hey, Yo! What the fuck are you doing Terry?" Reggie asked, while yanking Terry off of Vivian.

"I was fixin' to kill this bitch if you hadn't pulled me off of her ass. She's fucking this boxing bastard in my house, and then she turns around and tells me when I should stop beatin' his ass. She's got a lotta nerve. I'll tell you that."

Reggie made his way over to Vivian to see if she was alright. He placed his left hand on her shoulder and helped her to her feet. Vivian was in bad shape. Her neck was covered with reddish-purple marks from being strangled. Traumatized by the attack, her body twitched involuntarily.

He was glad he entered the room when he did or this might've been a double homicide. Terry shocked Vivian and Reggie with the brutal assault he manifested. He knew Simon, a professional boxer, would agree only if he was conscious.

Reggie told Terry that from here on it was important for him to be in control of his emotions. He would be of no help to his mission locked up for murder. Terry understood.

The two friends had to figure out how they could keep this ordeal from getting out. Simon and Vivian would need medical attention. Strangely enough Simon came to. He was the one who came up with a plausible explanation for what they'd tell the hospital workers when he and Vivian both showed up injured. He would say that he and Vivian had coincidentally met in Manhattan and she called upon him to help her carry the multitude of shopping bags she had back to her Vernon, New Jersey home. He didn't think it was a problem because she was a fan of his that he had met at a recent fight.

He'd say that at Vivian's home, once he put the bags down in the living room, she offered him a drink. That's when he was jumped from behind and beaten with a floor lamp and Vivian was strangled. The only reason neither of them was murdered was the siren of a local police car driving by the house panicked the invaders and they ran off. He would claim that they had on ski masks so they never saw their faces.

"Sounds good," Terry said. "But why?"

"Why what?"

"Why are you doing this? You could be arrested."

"He's engaged to Miss Michigan," Vivian confessed. "And if it ever got out that the heavyweight champion of the world was involved in an adulterous-fueled, violent altercation with the husband of the woman he was having an affair with...well, you know the rest. His reputation and career would be ca-ca."

"Go now, get outta here," instructed Simon rubbing his sore neck. "We'll handle it."

Back in New York, a weary Von Mickva arrived at his St. Moritz Hotel room at the twilight hour. He was escorted by three U.S. Marshals. He didn't know how long he could hold up against the pressure. The ongoing negotiations between the Baron and the U.S. Attorney to stave off a federal indictment broke down with more talks slated for the next morning. Von Mickva was exhausted and couldn't think of anything better than a hot shower and a good night sleep. He triggered the shower remotely and threw his keys on the credenza in the suite's foyer.

As he was about to turn in he received a phone call. It was his estranged wife, Sophie, who had moved out of Von Mickva's Sussex mansion four years ago and had since taken up with Sir John Hull, a distinguished member of London's parliament.

Sophie notified the Baron that he would receive divorce papers, via Federal Express, within twenty four to forty eight hours and that he should strongly consider signing them. She also said that if he didn't want to be fair in terms of the settlement, that he should know that she had already retained high-powered British divorce barrister Thomas Lloyd to make sure she "got what she was entitled to as a faithful partner in an overwhelming, arduous marriage of seventeen years."

Arduous? The Baron didn't feel their marriage had been arduous. Oh, there had been four separations and four reconciliations, alcohol binges-accompanied by threats of violence, and a bevy of girls that subsequently led to Sophie being infected with gonorrhea. Not to mention the numerous lawsuits brought on by fighters who felt they received far less than their contractual agreements.

The Baron smiled, admitting to himself that his marriage had been a wild ride. Once Sophie hung up abruptly, Von Mickva said out loud, "That bitch wants to rob me."

He called his lawyer, Milton Cosgrave.

"What can I do for you, Baron?"

"Sophie just called."

"What did she want?"

"A divorce."

"I can't say that I'm surprised."

"What's that supposed to mean?"

"Oh, come on, Baron do I have to spell it out for you?"

"Yes. I think you should."

Cosgrave was afraid Von Mickva would say that, but in any case, he proceeded.

"You know what type of relationship we've had. I've been your lawyer for twenty years and I've known Sophie ever since you married her seventeen years ago. I'm going to be frank with you...she's a sweet woman and I care for her dearly. And if I might say so, you've mistreated her at every turn."

Cosgrave's assessment drew angered silence from Von Mickva. The Baron composed himself and said, "Protect my affairs. She wants a sizable chunk of the pie. Make sure she gets the least she's entitled to," the Baron said before hanging up the telephone.

The Baron rested his head back on the black leather royal armchair he was sitting in. The chair was positioned just opposite a closet door that he suddenly noticed was opened. As he pondered the idea of rising up and crossing the Italian marble floor to check it out, a lone projectile whizzed through the closet, boring a hole through Von Mickva's skull just above his right ear.

His body and face froze. His hands were locked into a clawing position gripping the arms of the chair. His eyes took on a blankness reserved for convicted felons as they hear a jury of their peers return a sentence of death. It took less the two and a half seconds for Von Mickva to slump to his left and fall to the floor-knocking over the telephone with his left hand.

Now, there would be no plea bargain to discuss in the morning.

CHAPTER ELEVEN

Three Men In Dark Suites...Don't Think It's Pizza Delivery

The hunter green hills of Sussex, England provided a picturesque, yet somber atmosphere for the fifty two-car caravan following the black BMW hearse carrying the body of Baron Von Mickva from Crescent Church to Tavish Cemetery.

The cloudy, gray sky hovered over the procession as it snaked along the winding highway that led them toward the final resting place of a prolific fight promoter and investor of political upheaval.

Twenty four huge tents were set up inside the cemetery to protect family and friends from the constant patter of rain drenching the burial ceremony.

Sophie Von Mickva greeted mourners and accepted condolences as she stood next to the new man in her life, Sir John Hull. When the sympathies became too overwhelming, she clutched Hull's hand for support and resumed acknowledging the guests.

"I can't believe I'm here," Reggie said as he sat between Terry and Jaco.

"Why?" Jaco inquired.

"Because I just talked to him and I was with him over a week ago," Jaco remembered.

"Well, shit happens," Jaco said. "Shit happens."

"You didn't appear shocked at all, Jaco," Terry stated.

"Well...I don't wanna get into it...at least not now. We're supposed to be here for the man so let's be here for him," Jaco replied.

Terry and Reggie looked at each other, both friends searching the other's eyes for answers to Jaco's awkward demeanor.

The priest offered a brief ceremony and allowed family and close friends to tearfully eulogize Von Mickva. Despite the rain, several attendees shared their favorite Baron stories and the group laughed out loud until another person interjected with yet another funny story about the Baron.

"Come with me," Reggie said, taping Jaco on his shoulder.

"Where?" Jaco asked.

"We need to speak privately," Reggie answered.

"Okay, what's up?" Jaco said after quickly surveying the cemetery to see if anyone was observing them.

"You've been with the Baron for ump-tenth years, right?" Reggie asked.

"That's right."

"But you seem somewhat detached from the funeral and how everyone else is feeling," Reggie observed.

Terry was silent and trying to read the expression on Jaco's face.

"You think I'm happy about the Baron's death?"

"I'm not sure," Reggie answered.

"Well, I'm not. I'm really torn up over this. You gotta believe me," Jaco answered.

"Who would want him dead?" Terry asked.

"It's complicated," Jaco said.

"What do you mean it's complicated?" Terry shot back.

"He's been doing business for twenty six years. It's very likely that at least one or two of his past business associates felt resentment, animosity and contempt toward the Baron," Jaco pointed out.

"Is this gonna fuck up what we're doing?" Reggie inquired, stepping toward Jaco.

"I hope not," Jaco answered bluntly.

"You hope not?" Jaco repeated. "Well, that's comforting."

"What the hell is Strobe Nix doing here?" Jaco said, observing Nix as he walked toward the burial site.

Looking in the same direction as Jaco, Terry noticed the three men in dark suits heading towards Von Mickva's casket, which was propped above a pre-dug grave next to a large mound of dirt.

"Who's Strobe Nix?" Terry probed.

"Strobe Nix is an assistant U.S. attorney for the Eastern District of New York. He had a preliminary informal meeting with the Baron."

"What's that mean?" Reggie asked.

"A preliminary informal meeting is a meeting U.S. attorneys have with individuals before they are indicted to allow them to ponder a plea bargain."

"Was Von Mickva planning to squawk or fight?" Terry asked.

"Von Mickva wasn't a fight promoter for nothing. He too had been a pugilist in his youth. He told me once that his intension was to fight any indictment with every ounce of strength he had," Jaco confirmed.

Reggie, Terry and Jaco observed Nix and the other two men glaring down at the Baron's flower-draped casket as if he was the one that got away. After the men spoke to each other, they turned, walked up the hill and exited the cemetery.

"Hey, Jaco you think the Baron was murdered by business associates who thought he might cooperate with the government?" Terry asked.

"That's a possible scenario but I wouldn't worry about it. Reggie, you got your seed money, so your mission keeps rolling on," Jaco stated.

"Yeah, but what if Von Mickva already talked to the Feds?" Terry asked.

"Ain't nothing you can do about that now...but if you get a knock at the door, don't think that it's pizza delivery," Jaco answered insightfully.

That type of thinking really worried Reggie because he was already well aware of what was brewing between the Baron and the government. What wasn't certain was to what degree Von Mickva had or was intending to cooperate. The forecast was unknown, like jumping off a diving board and not knowing if the water was hot or cold.

CHAPTER TWELVE

A Reason for Caring

Reggie finally woke up after sleeping for hours when he returned home to The Cottonwood.

The flight from England was long and boring. But to add insult to injury, the plane circled the airport for two hours due to low visibility, increasing the length of the flight to ten hours.

After a long, hot shower, he scheduled a 4:00 p.m. meeting with Skip, the three men Skip had recommended for the mission, Jaco and Terry. The plan was to give the guys a chance to get acquainted and to go over logistics and duties.

Before the meeting, Reggie had four hours to unplug his ears, to enjoy a brandy and to jot down relevant points of intent to be conveyed to the team. He was a little irritated when he was interrupted by the phone ringing, but he answered it anyway.

"Hello?"

"What's up baby?" Sylvia cooed.

"Sylvia, why are you calling me? I'm busy right now," Reggie said in a deadpan voice.

"You don't have any time for your best girl?" Sylvia asked using a silky tone.

"No, I don't. What's this all about?" Reggie asked, sucking his teeth irreverently.

"It's about us silly...who else?" Sylvia replied. "But, I have an absolutely fabulous idea..."

"I can't wait to hear this," Reggie said, crossing his feet on the coffee table.

"Are you sitting down?"

"Yes."

"Why don't we...get married again?" she said, speaking very slowly.

"You can't be serious."

"Oh, can't I?"

"Come on, now. We went through this before. I certainly don't think it would be any better the second time around."

"Oh, you don't think so? Why?"

"Because, mentally, I'm somewhere else. I'm on a road unparalleled by any path you've ever traveled on."

"What the hell are you talking about, Reggie?"

"I got some shit to do and I won't be able to focus on anything else until I complete my task."

"Which is?"

"Oh, no. I'm not discussing that with you."

"And why not?"

"Because it's none of your business, that's why."

"You don't have to be rude, Reggie. I was just expressing how I feel about you, Baby," she said, leaving an awkward pregnant pause between them and then whispering harshly, "I love you. Is that a crime?"

"No. No, it's not a crime. But you're trying to resurrect a relationship that can never be restored to its pure, original form. So much has occurred that we would appear desperate for the effort. We need to move on and find new loves."

Reggie's response collapsed the walls in the coffee house where Sylvia was sitting. She felt so alone and distant from her reality, which comprised forty two other coffee house patrons who all seemed to be enjoying themselves. While they were laughing, conversing with one another, ordering coffees, lattes, various muffins, breads and pastries in a symphony of consumption, she sat frozen in a sea of rejection.

Reggie placed a large pillow from the sofa between his knees. He was still holding the phone, but wondered silently why Sylvia would offer up such a terrible idea. He knew that, if agreed upon, their relationship would roll on until the wheels fell off and then breakdown again. Reggie didn't have the strength, motivation or endurance to put forth the effort.

"Are you there? He asked. "Sylvia, are you there?"

Sylvia remained silent, lost in her own thoughts.

"Sylvia?"

Ambient sounds registered through Reggie's ears until he wondered whether Sylvia had passed out or simply walked away from her cell phone. Suddenly a strange voice spoke into the phone.

"Is someone on the other end of the line?" a foreign voice bellowed.

"Who is this?" Reggie asked. "Who is this?"

"It's Kyle."

"Who?"

"Kyle."

"Am I supposed to know you?" Reggie asked.

"If you've been to Minks and ordered a Montana Mountain Espresso I probably made it for you," the voice said.

"Okay," Reggie said. "But where is the proprietor of the cell phone you're talking on?"

"Oh, Sylvia...she walked out and left it on the table. She must've really had something on her mind to walk out of here and forget to take her cell phone with her."

"Yeah, well I've been known to have that effect on people."

"Yeah? Who are you anyway?"

"Nobody. I'm nobody, Kid," Reggie said before promptly hanging up the phone.

The kid, still holding the cell phone against his ear, looked towards the window and front door where Sylvia had exited hoping to spot her re-entering the coffee shop. No Sylvia in sight.

Little did he know, but Sylvia was across the street in the gas station bathroom. She was crouched in a fetal position with her hands balled up in a fist pressed against her eyes. Tears leaked out from behind her wrists and cascaded down her cheeks. The hopes of ever fulfilling her dream to renew her matrimonial union with Mr. Reggie Cochran were deflated.

Reggie struggled with his feelings, too. He held Sylvia in high regard. In fact, he still loved her. He just couldn't imagine taking on the responsibility of a relationship while working to fulfill his mission.

All he really wanted to do at the moment was to eat and wait for his team to arrive. He had been looking forward to this meeting for a long, long time.

After scoffing down three hot dogs in rapid succession, Reggie polished off half a bottle of Merlot. Finally, his guests arrived and all at virtually the same time. The team was an all-star lineup of anti-establishment, nonconformist, who were licking their chops at the opportunity to sign up for the melee of the century.

In attendance were Otto Stoffler of Baader Meinhoff (Germany), Pepe Junot of Action Directe (France), Roberto Rios of Los Machateros (Puerto Rico), Jaco Philips of The Black Panthers (United States), Skip Raymond of the F.B.I. (United States) and Terry Williams along with Reggie Cochran to round out the group.

With snacks and refreshments served, Reggie answered everyone's concerns and then explained the plan. He told the team that New York State Parole Commissioners conduct parole hearings—also known as final hearings—every month at facilities throughout the prison system to determine which inmates are worthy for release to parole supervision. These hearings are commenced sixty days before scheduled releases. If an inmate hasn't involved himself in programs that are mandated and deemed necessary to justify a change in criminal thinking and behavior, the inmate will be denied parole and subsequently held over for conditional release-which is calculated as two thirds of their maximum sentence.

Reggie pitched his idea of dressing up as New York State Department of Highway workers on the job fixing a road near Clinton Correction Facility-the place of his incarceration and the cancer in his soul. A detour will be set up to veer the parole commissioners onto a secluded road where the faux highway workers will ambush their van, kidnap them and murder the driver-a State Correction Officer.

"Sounds like a winner," Ross said.

"This is gonna be fun," Jaco said.

"It seems that all seven men were in collective agreement about the feasibility of success regarding the assignment.

"Don't get me wrong," Otto Stoffler said, in an effort to be crystal clear about his position, "I'm here for the money but why are you going after these three people so tenaciously?"

"It's because they destroyed my kindness, my humanity, my dignity and lastly, my inspiration," Reggie said. "I couldn't comprehend why my brother was set up to look like he had accepted a bribe. He was just doing his job. He was only following the law. To see Vincent in court every day—to watch his spirit and his self-respect slowly drained out of him—really hurt me," Reggie added, his voice cracking with emotion. "Vincent had always been a great big brother. I looked up to him. I still do. But the New York State Division of Parole kept sentencing me over and over again because of the notoriety of my case. And for that, they will pay dearly. What would you have done if it was your brother?" he asked without waiting for an answer. "And to top it off, David Markoff never did one day in jail. Is that fair? Where is the justice?

"Well, if I wasn't convinced of your resolve before, now I understand why you're doing this," Roberto said. "I got your back, Bro," he added, shaking Reggie's hand with sincerity as he prepared to leave the meeting.

CHAPTER THIRTEEN

The Commencement

The gate to Comstock Correctional Facility opened uneventfully. A gray van featuring the New York State seal on its side doors barreled passed the guard's booth and onto the road.

Thomas Boyle, Lou DeMello and Cindy Howarth rode nonchalantly in the back seats amidst their legal file briefcases and lunch bags. Two correctional officers sat in the front. One drove while the other provided security.

"What are you so happy about?" Cindy Howarth asked after observing a slight smirk on Thomas Boyle's face.

"Yeah, I've never seen you this jovial," Lou DeMello affirmed.

"One hundred and seventy eight parole hearings and only ninety seven released to parole," Boyle announced proudly.

"And you're happy about that?" Howarth inquired.

"Of course...that means eighty one maggots won't be leaving their cages," Boyle replied with a chuckle.

"I can't even believe I know you," Cindy said, shaking her head.

Boyle continued to smile even broader as he clutched his briefcase.

The driver and his partner were surprised by a series of new Men at Work, Work Zone and Slow

Down road signs. A truck placed before a Y-turn forced the correctional department van to make a left turn instead of a right.

"You guys ready? Reggie asked from inside the truck facing the Y-turn.

"Yeah!" Pepe Junot said.

"You know I live for this shit," said Otto Stoffler.

Arranging his tool belt so that his 45 cal. Remington remained concealed, Jaco responded by nodding his head in the affirmative.

"Gentlemen, have you ever seen people headed to their death?" Reggie asked as the van containing the three doomed State employees passed them by. "Well, there they go. Wave goodbye."

"Why are those road workers waving at us?" Lou DeMello asked, apparently miffed by the highway workers salutation.

"I don't know. Maybe they're just friendly," Cindy said.

"Don't be silly," Thomas Boyle replied. "They're just a bunch of asshole road workers."

Cindy Howarth just shook her head, "You're so unbelievable," she said.

Skip, Terry and Roberto were in another truck two blocks away awaiting the correctional van's appearance for Phase Two. They had created the perfect diversion as State Highway workers blocking access to the other side of a carefully designated street.

Once the van was followed in by the truck driven by Reggie, Jaco, Pepe and Otto, the parole commissioners were trapped. Otto leaped from the truck, firing a semiautomatic with great accuracy, killing both officers instantly. The blood-splattered and terrified parole commissioners huddled together in the back of the van, screaming until their voices broke. They struggled to crawl under the seats, clawing and groping for an escape.

Reggie stepped down from the truck followed by Pepe and Jaco. Each man walked slowly toward the disabled vehicle. Skip, Terry and Roberto were already standing on the left side of the van. Cochran peeped into the back window of the van and smiled.

"Please don't kill me," Howarth shrieked.

"What did we do? What did we do?" Boyle shouted.

"Shut the fuck up and wait for orders!" Pepe yelled.

Nothing could measure the level of fear going through the minds of the commissioners at the sight of Reggie, Pepe, Otto, Jaco, Skip, Terry and Roberto surrounding the van, armed to the teeth.

"What's this all about?" DeMello shouted as he lifted his head slightly above the frame of the van's shot-out windows.

An eerie silence fell over the road as DeMello's hysteria went unanswered. No one seemed to breathe as the team stood there, staring at the three victims-to-be.

"I'm glad you didn't get too excited and kill all three of our guests, Otto," Reggie said. "That's *my* job."

Reggie slid open the van's side door and said with a huge grin, "Remember me?"

"No. Who are you?" DeMello asked, poking his head out slowly to get a closer look. "Sh-sh-should I know you?" he stammered.

"Damn right you should," Reggie retorted, casually resting his arm around Skip's shoulder. "It's not every day that you get to meet two people that you've had sex with."

Puzzled by the reply, DeMello returned, "I-I-I've never had sex with any of you because I'm, I'm not gay."

"You may not be gay, but the three of you have definitely fucked us!" Skip replied, placing his two hands on DeMello's cheeks and roughly squeezing them together.

As Reggie detailed the intricacies of both his and Skip's cases, the three commissioners began to pale and were dripping with perspiration.

In her panic, Cindy Howarth suddenly remembered how she had often discussed with her co-workers the possibility of retaliation by parolees still disgruntled after being released. Frightened by this likelihood, Cindy had recently made the decision to resign and return to graduate school. But now, it was too late.

Reggie instructed Pepe and Otto to put the three terrified and just flex cuffed parole commissioners into a strategically located van parked across the street from the ambush site. Jaco, Skip, Terry and Roberto quickly made their way to another van parked behind the vehicle the commissioners were placed in.

While driving to the chateau, the commissioners pleaded with their captors to be released. They incessantly begged for answers about why they were being kidnapped. Reggie didn't utter a word. He kept the suspense tight and the held their fear even tighter during the entire trip. The van finally came to a stop about an hour and forty minutes later when they pulled into the long, winding driveway leading up to the chateau.

"What is this place? DeMello asked.

"Think of it as a home away from home," Reggie replied, laughing dryly.

The bright afternoon sun gleaming off the fine crystals embedded into the chateau's cream-colored limestone exterior created a picturesque view against the lush, green New York State background. After undergoing considerable and precise renovations under Reggie's direction, the chateau was revived to its original, castle-like splendor. The chateau's classic gothic architecture and its mountaintop location, was as foreboding as a prison.

The three commissioners were led inside. Cindy Howarth's heel broke when she tripped on the brushed stone driveway. She fell to the ground and immediately attempted to scurry away on her hands and knees. Skip amused himself for a moment by watching her futile escape attempt. Then he grabbed her around the waist and lifted her to her feet. DeMello and Boyle eyed each other as if to indicate that there was nothing either of them could do to come to Cindy's aid. They simply kept trudging somberly towards the chateau at gunpoint.

Once inside, they were led into an elevator adjacent to the massive kitchen to a basement area. The ride to the lower level was unusually long. Much to

Reggie's delight, the frigid basement was twenty feet below ground level.

Boyle hesitated before exiting the elevator.

"Please, please, man. Whatever you want, I'll get it. Whatever you need from me, I'm willing to do it," he said, pleading in a high-pitched tone, before dropping to his knees and clasping his hands in a prayer-like position in front of his face. "Just let me live," he cried, spit drooling out of the corners of his mouth. "Just let me live."

"Man, get your punk ass up!" Reggie ordered. "You made my life a living hell. You made my brother's life a living hell. And to top it off, you cultivated your own star chamber in Albany—deciding who would be released and who would be denied their freedom—according to *your* own fucked up ideology.

"No. No. I didn't mean to do that. I'm begging you," Boyle stammered as Howarth and DeMello looked on tearfully.

"If you don't believe in God I suggest that you start now," Reggie answered, as he gave the signal to his team to continue moving the three commissioners into their respective rooms in the basement.

The commissioners were led down a long, stark white hallway. Though scrubbed and swept, this area of the chateau had not undergone the upgrades Reggie had made to the rest of the house. The paint on the cinderblock walls and ceiling was badly peeling and an old-fashioned radiator stood in front of a barred window at the end of the hall. Three freshly painted doors stood along the wall opposite the elevator. Each door was painted with a large number one, two and three on it.

Pepe and Otto escorted Cindy Howarth to *Room One,* bedecked with a stainless steel mortuary gurney furnished with selected tools and syringes.

Jaco and Skip ushered Thomas Boyle to *Room Two,* outfitted with a barber's chair with four thick leather restraints and a metal basin positioned between two footprint makers painted on the floor where a person's feet could be placed.

Terry and Roberto escorted Lou DeMello to *Room Three*, which was equipped with a stainless steel stool that had a seven inch hole in the seat. The stool was lined up directly below a seven inch hole in the ground.

Once the three parole commissioners were strapped in, Reggie entered *Room One.*

"You may not know why you're here, but it doesn't matter now. You have been held over for a final hearing to determine the validity of the crimes you have committed against those who are incarcerated and seeking release to freedom," he said, his voice echoing throughout the room.

"What? No-no-no. Why do you believe that? Cindy Howarth screamed hysterically, "I was only doing my job."

Reggie wagged his index finger in front of her nose as she lay flat on the gurney.

"You were led to believe that you were protecting the people of the State of New York, but in actuality you were sealing your fate," he said, bending to look her in the eye. "With your shield and your sword you go about your job as if you're some moral crusader doling out judgment on those already judged."

Reggie slowly stood up and walked over to an old wooden table attached at the foot of the gurney. He lifted a dirty blue oblong case, which contained ten fully-loaded syringes. He unzipped the case to expose each extra-long needle.

"What are you going to do with those things?"

"They my dear...are for you."

Cindy began hyperventilating. Her body shook uncontrollably and her chest was heaving in convulsion. Her eyes bulged as Reggie walked toward her with his hands behind his back.

"Have you ever heard of Pavulon, Ms. Howarth?"

"Help! Help me!" Cindy shrieked. "What is that? Is that what's in those needles?" she screamed, struggling wildly to break her restraints.

"It's a muscle relaxer most often used as anesthesia during surgery," Reggie explained. "But since the re-emergence of the death penalty—specifically lethal injection—Pavulon has been one of the primary ingredients of the deadly cocktail. Personally, I prefer to use it alone at 50 times its legal limit—which slows the heart rate to a crawl, so you literally suffocate from inside," he said, smiling. "What a way to go out, huh?" Reggie said smiling explosively in front of Cindy Howarth's tear-drenched face.

Reggie opened the case and pulled out one of the syringes. He grabbed her right arm and with the needle in his right hand aimed for the pit of her arm. She wriggled in an attempt to knock the needle away, but Reggie unceremoniously plunged the needle into her skin and squeezed the powerful drug into her arm.

"Please you don't have to do this," Cindy cried out.

"It's already done, Ms. Howarth. Bye-bye."

Within seconds, the Pavulon began lowering Cindy's blood pressure and heart rate. Her breathing became shallow and her eyes converted to tiny slits leaking tears that rolled down the side of her face and onto the gurney. Cindy Howarth left this world and entered a place that no one alive had ever visited before.

Otto and Pepe walked out of the room ahead of Reggie.

"I've done some brutal shit in the past, but what just went on in there even caused me to pause," Otto confessed to Reggie.

"Me too," Pepe said. "Reggie, man, you were all business in there."

Reggie shook the hands of Otto and Pepe and moved on to Room Two.

Thomas Boyle sat in *Room Two*, strapped to a barber chair secured by four thick leather restraints. His feet were inside a wide pot with a water tube inserted in the left side.

Reggie put both hands on Commissioner Boyle's shaking knees to still them.

"Do you know why you're here?" he asked.

"No, but if you know what's good for you, you better let me go I know that!" Boyle said, crying.

Reggie allowed an awkward silence to settle in the room. He bent to stare eye-to-eye with Boyle.

"Or what? You're gonna kick my ass or something?" he asked sarcastically. "You gonna take me outside and show me a thing or two?"

Skip and Jaco looked on as Boyle squeezed his eyes tightly, yielding to Reggie's clear power and authority in this situation.

"You have been held over for a final hearing to determine the validity of the crimes you have committed against those who are incarcerated and seeking their release to freedom."

"Why are you doing this to me?" Boyle blubbered like a beaten bully. "I haven't done anything to you."

"You were led to believe that you were protecting the people of the State of New York but in actuality you were sealing your fate. With your shield and your sword you go about your job as if you're some moral crusader doling out judgment on those already judged."

"Is this some sort of nightmare or something?

"If it is, you better wake up," Reggie said, as he pushed a button on the wall before continuing, "because it's about to go down."

"Wh-what happens when you push that button?" Boyle asked.

"You'll soon notice the pot your feet are in will begin filling with water. But it's the plate below the pot that you should be worried about."

"Wh-wh-why?" Boyle stammered.

"It will heat to an excruciating boil that will melt your skin and have you screaming decibels far, far above anything you've ever uttered in your life."

Boyles' eyes bulged as he watched water snaking through the Plexiglas tube toward an opening in the pot. When the vessel filled to within an inch from the top, the hot plate began to heat the water to a boil. Boyle's toes began to wrinkle and his skin subsequently began to peel off his feet. Boyle shook violently, trying to break free, but the restraints were so tight that all he could muster was a series of intense, guttural screams.

"Hell will get you Reggie Cochran!" he cried, exhausted from screaming.

"Not before I see you die," Reggie said, pulling a 9mm. from his waistband and firing two bullets that pierced Boyle's forehead. The Commissioner's body fell limp, his feet still boiling in the pan of water.

Finally, Reggie entered Room Three, where Lou DeMello was seated naked below the waist. The Commissioner had been placed on a stainless steel stool.

"You may not know why you're here," Reggie said repeating the speech he gave the prior two victims, "but it doesn't matter now. You have been held over for a final hearing to determine the validity of the crimes you have committed against those who are incarcerated and seeking release to their freedom."

"You killed them didn't you?" DeMello asked.

Reggie remained silent.

"You did...you killed them and now you here to get rid of me," Lou said, his eyes swollen from the repeated tears he had already shed.

"You know, Commissioner DeMello, my mother always told me to the point whenever I tried explaining something to her. Ironically, you're sitting on the point, the point of an eight and a half inch iron pole, sharpened at the tip."

Pepe, Otto, Jaco, Skip, Terry and Roberto slowly backed away, moving to a position in the back of the room.

"I'm going to give you a chance to live."

"I want my clothes back. Why did you remove my pants?"

"Because I'm humiliating you, that's why," Reggie said, laughing wickedly.

"What do I have to do?" DeMello asked.

"I'm going to ask you a question and if you answer correctly, you're free to go," Reggie replied.

"That's it?" DeMello asked.

"That's it."

"I don't believe that you wielded any power over Boyle and Howarth when they decided who to release to parole supervision," Reggie explained. "I think you just went along with the majority."

"My vote was always independent and free of pressure from my co-board members," DeMello said as if he had rehearsed this speech for just such an occasion.

"Oh really?" Reggie asked. "Well give me the names of five people that you argued contrary to your colleagues vote to deny release to parole?"

DeMello's mind began racing to find an answer to Reggie's question.

"You can start right now," Reggie said, beginning the countdown. "Ten...nine..."

Lou looked up towards the ceiling, hoping to find the names of five people he had argued to have released against his fellow board members' decision to deny.

"...eight...seven...six...," Reggie continued.

Reggie gazed over DeMello's slumped shoulder and winked at his team members. He just knew DeMello couldn't come up with any names.

"...five...four...three..."

Dripping tears and sweat, Lou struggled to come up with the names that would free him from annihilation.

"...two...one. I knew you couldn't do it," Reggie said.

"Wait! Wait! I need more time."

"We all need more time," Reggie said. "We need more time to right our wrongs—more time to sing our favorite songs. Too bad we can never say the days are too long."

The sound of a mechanism emanating from below his stool startled DeMello.

"What's that noise?" he screamed.

"Oh, that," Reggie said laughing. "I meant to tell you about that. You're sitting on a stool with a hole in the seat. That hole lines up perfectly with the hole in the floor. That hole has an eight foot rod with a sharpened edge that will impale you right through your rectum.

"Oh God...when?"

"The process has already started," Reggie said, "once I counted down to one. What you heard was the rod moving towards your body. You'll feel something in just a moment."

DeMello screamed, as the metal pole moved through the stool, into his body-puncturing muscles, organs and arteries. Finally, its point emerged from the top of his skull and splattered blood all over Reggie's face and shirt, bathing him in shards of his enemy's anatomy.

Each of Reggie's team members looked away from the grisly scene. The steel shaft prevented DeMello's red-glazed, limp and lifeless body from falling to the floor. Reggie, splattered with blood, smiled and wiped his face with the back of his hand. In a sick kind of Hannibal Lecter way, he was proud to wear the blood of his victim and stood back to admire the carnage.

Moments later, the team swiftly exited the chateau of slaughter. Each man left in a separate taxi and headed to a different airport—LaGuardia and John F. Kennedy Airports in New York City, Westchester County Airport, Newark and Teterboro Airports in New Jersey and Central Islip Airport in Long Island—never to see each other again.

Reggie's explicit instructions regarding the exit strategy were that everyone was to make separate travel arrangements. He didn't want any of the team members to know where any of the others was going. He wanted to be sure that no one was able to divulge the whereabouts of the others if, by chance, anyone was caught.

While he waited for his flight at the airport, Reggie received a phone call. It was Vincent. He called to beg Reggie to not kill those parole commissioners.

"Everything is alright now, Bro. We can finally relax. See you soon Vinnie. See you soon."

...To Be Continued.

About The Author

Oscar Sanders is an award winning director of short, feature films, and music videos. Currently, he has been focusing on feature jazz documentaries-his last about the life and musical dynamics of award winning composer/violinist entitled Billy Bang: Long Over Due garnered awards in the USA and Europe. His upcoming project is another feature documentary about jazz icon/master drummer Michael Carvin entitled Michael Carvin: No Excuses.

www.malcolmentertainment.com

Oscar Sanders is available for select reading and lectures. To inquire about possible appearances please email at malcolmentertainment@yahoo.com or call 718-924-5873